The Christian Way of Living

Klaus Bockmuehl

REGENT COLLEGE PUBLISHING
VANCOUVER, BRITISH COLUMBIA

The Christian Way of Living

The Christian Way of Living

Copyright © 1994, Elisabeth Bockmuehl

Originally published as, *Christliche Lebensfuhrung*
© 1994 Brunnen Verlag Giessen

Reproduced 1998 by Regent College Publishing, an imprint of the Regent College Bookstore, 5800 University Boulevard, Vancouver, B.C. V6T 2E4
email: bookstore@regent-college.edu
Website: www.regent-bookstore.com
Orders toll-free: 1-800-663-8664

The views expressed in this work are those of the author and do not necessarily represent the official position of Regent College.

Printed On-Demand in the United States of America

All rights reserved. No part of this publication may be reproduced, stored in a retrieval system, or transmitted, in any form or by any means, electronic, mechanical, photocopying, recording of otherwise, without the prior written permission of the author, except in the case of brief quotations embodied in critical articles and reviews.

Library of Congress Cataloging-in-Publication Data

Bockmühl, Klaus, *(1931-1989)*
   The Christian way of living:
      an ethics of the ten commandments

   147 p. 22 cm.
   Includes bibliographical references.
   1. Ten commandments -- addresses, essays, lectures.
   2. Ten commandments -- criticism, interpretation, etc.
   3. Ten commandments -- meditations   I. Title
BV4655.B624   1994

ISBN 1-57383-023-2

The Christian Way of Living

An Ethics of the Ten Commandments

From the same author:
> *Listening to the God who Speaks*
> *The Challenge of Marxism*
> *Evangelicals and Social Action*
> *Living by the Gospel*
> *The Unreal God of Modern Theology*

Contents:

Foreword ix

Introduction to Ethics
What is Ethics? 1
Why Study Ethics? 2
The Place of Ethics in Theology 5

Introduction to the Decalogue

A. The Decalogue in the Bible 7
1. Institution 7
2. The Function of the Decalogue in the Old Testament 8
3. The Reaffirmation and Interpretation of the Decalogue in the New Testament 9

B. The Decalogue in the History of the Teaching of the Church 11
1. The First Two Centuries 11
2. The Church Fathers 12
3. The Recovery of the Decalogue during the Middle Ages 15
4. The Decalogue in the Reformation (Luther & Calvin) 15
5. Modernity 18

C. The Hermeneutics of the Decalogue 20
1. Method of Exposition 20
2. Applications of the Decalogue 22
3. The Place of the Decalogue in a System of Christian Ethics 23
4. Appendix on the Counting of the Commandments 27

The First Commandment
A. Exposition 29
1. The Negative Version in the Old Testament 29
2. The Negative Version in the New Testament 31
3. The Positive Version in the Old Testament 31
4. The Positive Version in the New Testament 32

B. A Meditation on the Functions of the Commandments 33
1. The Critical Function 33
2. The Liberating Function 34
3. The Commanding Function 36

C. The Love of God as the Central Content of the Commandments 37
1. The Loss of the Love of God in the History of Theology 37
2. God's Love for Man 39
3. Man's Love for God 43
    The Love of God in Paul 45
    Two Practical Applications 46

The Second Commandment
A. Exposition 51
1. The Negative Version in the Old Testament 51
2. The Negative Version in the New Testament 53
3. The Positive Version in the Old Testament 53
4. The Positive Version in the New Testament 54

B. Meditiation on the Prohibition of Imagery 56

The Third Commandment
A. Exposition 59
1. The Negative Version in the Old Testament 59
    Avoiding the Name 60
2. The Negative Version in the New Testament 61
3. The Positive Version in the Old Testament 62
4. The Positive Version in the New Testament 62

B. The Meaning of the Third Commandment 64
1. Reformation Interpretation 64
2. What the Commandment Means Today 65
3. An Appendix on Taking an Oath 65

The Fourth Commandment
A. Exposition 69
1. *The Positive Version in the Old Testament* 70
2. *The Negative Version in the Old Testament* 72
3. *The Fourth Commandment in the New Testament* 74

B. Traditional Exposition in Christianity 76
The Horizons of the Christian Sabbath 78

The Fifth Commandment
A. Exposition 79
1. *The Negative Version in the Old Testament* 79
2. *The Positive Version in the Old Testament* 80
3. *The Parent-Child Relationship in the New Testament.* 81
4. *The Eschatological Relativization of the Natural Family* 83
5. *The Constitution of the New Family of Believers* 84
6. *The Transfiguration of the Natural Family* 85

B. Present-day Problems in the Field of
Parent-Child Relationships 85

C. Other Relationships of Authority and Subordination 86
1. *Authority and Subordination in Work and Business* 86
2. *Authority and Liberation in the Church* 87
3. *The Christian and the State: Authority and Subordination in Politics* 88

The Sixth Commandment
A. Exposition 93
1. *The Negative Version in the Old Testament* 93
2. *The Negative Version in the New Testament* 94
3. *The Positive Version in the Old Testament* 94
4. *The Positive Version in the New Testament* 94

B. Three Contemporary Issues: Abortion, Euthanasia and Suicide 96
1. *Abortion* 96
2. *Euthanasia* 100
3. *Suicide* 100

The Seventh Commandment
A. Exposition 103
1. The Negative Version in the Old Testament 103
2. The Negative Version in the New Testament 105
3. The Positive Version in the Old Testament 107
4. The Positive Version in the New Testament 108

The Eight Commandment
A. Exposition 111
1. The Negative Version in the Old Testament 111
2. The Negative Version in the New Testament 112
   Motivation in the Old and New Testaments 112
3. The Positive Version in the Old Testament 113
4. The Positive Version in the New Testament 114

B. Reformational and Contemporary Exposition
on the Eight Commandment 115

The Ninth Commandment
A. Exposition 117
1. The Negative Version in the Old Testament 117
2. The Positive Version in the New Testament 118

B. The Interpretation of the Ninth Commandment
in the Catechisms 119

The Tenth Commandment
A. Exposition 121
1. The Negative Version in the Old Testament 121
2. The Negative Version in the New Testament 122
3. The Positive Version in the Old Testament 123
4. The Positive Version in the New Testament 123

Appendix:
The Ten Commandments: Are They Still Valid? 125

Author Index 137
Scripture Index 139
Subject Index 145

Foreword

A recent Regent graduate asked me to write an introduction to this book. Tom came too late to Regent to be able to study under my husband, but he had taken a video course of Klaus' lectures and was very inspired by some of his books as well as by the articles about my husband by Art Thomas (see *Crux*, March and June, 1993).

It is not easy to publish posthumous works for the simple reason that people prefer to buy books by living authors. So I admire the Regent Bookstore for their decision to take on the publication of this book. I am convinced that Klaus' approach to Christian ethics is not outdated. In a widely read German Christian magazine (*Idea*), there was a response to the German edition of this book by Peter Hahne, a well known TV reporter and theologian. I quote:

> "Yet another ethics? No, finally an ethics! Since A. Schlatter and Karl Heim, German Pietism has not produced a general description of Christian living. Today, ethics is marked by the relativization of biblical norms. Bockmuehl confronts this with an Ethics of the Ten Commandments. There is exegesis of the Old Testament and the New Testament correlations. Difficult passages are not avoided but dealt with courageously. ... This book is easy to comprehend and contains a unique compendium for responsible Christians."

Klaus often said he wanted to live and work for a renewal in theology and church, a return to the will of God, and Christian ethics had a central place for him in this dream. Actually, he called his course on the Ten Commandments "Basic Christian Ethics" (Ethics I), and he had in mind one day to write a continuation, an "Ethics II", which would mainly deal with topics like prayer, conversion, praise, Christian love - but this was not meant to be. Sometimes people classified Klaus as a legalistic person, but such people completely misunderstood him. Klaus was a spiritual person. He wanted all that he did and thought to reflect his love of the Lord — this was absolutely central in Klaus' life, as one can detect from the title of the memorial volume dedicated to Klaus, *Loving God and Keeping His Commandments* (*Gott lieben und seine Gebote halten*, Brunnen 1991). This book is bilingual as it contains German and English essays written by Klaus' friends, colleagues and former students, a reflection of Klaus' spiritual and theological legacy. There are about three of Klaus' posthumous works which will be published within the next few years, of which the *The Christian Way of Living* is the first. All of these three volumes will contain lecture material that Klaus had not yet prepared for publication. With the help of Klaus' last teaching assistant, Rev. Mark Buchanan, the final manuscript was put together. Very helpful in this process were the lecture notes of a former teaching assistant, Rory Rundell. I am especially grateful to Mark for the careful and diligent way in which he tried to edit the final manuscript. In the last stages of the editing Dr. Don Lewis' help was significant.

I am happy to help with making these posthumous writings available to the public. In a way, this is the continuation of the work I did for Klaus while he was alive. Klaus would always discuss his manuscripts with me while he was working on a project. At the same time I was involved in the process because I worked as his typist. Klaus wrote everything by putting pen to paper, he never typed on a typewriter or a computer. I enjoy very much to be part of his work again, especially as I translate these books into German.

Elisabeth Bockmuehl
Spring 1994, Vancouver

Introduction to Ethics

1. What is Ethics?

When attempting to define a term, it often helps to trace it back to its roots. However, this does not work with the term "ethics." The word comes from the Greek *ethos*, which means "custom" or "habit." It is similar to the Latin *mos*, which is the root of our word "morals" but which means, in its original usage, habitual or customary behaviour. Both these root terms lack the element of good versus evil which forms the basis of our concept of ethics and morals. Today, we use the term ethics generically to generally mean instruction in morals, in how we should live and act. Ethics is the science of right living.

In our day, ethics is not descriptive, but prescriptive: It tells us not how we live but how *to* live. This is an important distinction. The work of science is to make distinctions, to be precise. Precision and clarity are especially needed in an age such as ours, when idealogies and demagogues manipulate concepts by tampering with language and language categories. The first step to slavery is loss of language, when words are ransacked of their true and clear meanings and replaced with new and vague ones. We make ourselves easy prey to ideologies when we have fuzzy concepts and blurred definitions.

So we need to be precise and definite: Ethics is the teaching of what is correct human behaviour.

2. Why Study Ethics?

Ethics is frequently missing from the curricula of evangelical theological institutions. This is remarkable in view of the stern moralism and detailed regulation of behaviour among many evangelicals. Perhaps they think a course in ethics is superfluous. Perhaps evangelicals are so thoroughly indoctrinated within the family that they have no need to discuss ethics. Is ethics, in traditional (pre-1700) reformational style, included as a subsection in dogmatics (systematic theology) under the heading "good works"? Whatever the explanation for this omission, ethics should be taught as a separate subject in our theological institutions today. It is a crucial and much-needed subject of theological inquiry and Christian living.

There are two basic reasons for this. The first is an anthropological one: Ethics is needed because of the nature of man. We act out of sheer and simple necessity, to maintain life. And unlike the animals who act on instinct, we are capable of making decisions. Our lives are riddled with dilemmas and tangled in complexity, and we must continually ask the question which Peter's audience put to him: "What shall we do?" (Acts 2:37). This is a universal human question.

Friedrich Nietzsche—who was terribly hostile to Christianity—once shrewdly remarked that "Man is the incomplete animal." An animal's actions merely follow a pattern mapped out by instinct. But a man can and must choose a course. A man directs his own existence by his choices and actions. This is especially true for modern Western man, who is not preoccupied with food-gathering or with any other of the basic tasks of survival. Issues of survival are settled by breakfast, and so we have the rest of the day in which we are free, and perhaps compelled, to choose a way to live.

The second reason we need to study ethics is a specifically Christian one. It can be divided into three separate yet related parts. Firstly, God's intention for his redeemed people is to live in holiness. The purpose of salvation is the sanctification of the believer. "He gave himself for us to redeem us from all iniquity and to purify for himself a people of his own who are zealous for good works" (Tit. 2:14). Ethics answers the question, "What good works?"

Secondly, the study of ethics has an eschatological horizon. We face a last judgement, and are held responsible for what we have done (2 Cor. 5:10). Humanity lives between the poles of good and evil; we must choose, and then give an account for our choices.

Thirdly, we have an earthly horizon, the need to witness to our pagan surroundings. This was especially emphasized in the early church, but in our time has again become a key issue. The early church, embedded in Greco-Roman society, with its melee of cults and moral waywardness, had a clear sense of this need. Good works and purity of life were the distinguishing marks of the Christians, that which separated them from the surrounding pagan morality and mentality. Goodness and charity carry their own missionary appeal. This is especially evident in the second century apostolic fathers, who speak of a two-way scheme: a way of light and a way of darkness. The way of light is often understood as being staked out by the Ten Commandments. Today, the pluralism which characterized the time of the early church is once again prevalent, and once again there is a pressing need for Christians, through their way of life, both to distinguish themselves from and to witness to pagan society.

There are two further remarks needed to emphasize the relevance and timeliness of ethics for our time. These concern modern individualism and relativism. In the Middle Ages we find the "Holy Roman Empire" overarching and hemming in Western Christendom. In medieval Europe, most people were legally bound to Christianity. After the Reformation, Christianity in Europe was divided up according to the different confessions, either Catholic, Lutheran or Reformed. The people were bound to whatever confession their particular duke or prince held (*"Cuius regio eius religio"*, meaning "In the prince's country, the prince's religion"). Within each domain the old rules still applied thanks to the Peace of Augsburg (1555). In the beginning of the nineteenth century, the Holy Roman Empire was secularized, and so the source and centre of ethical instruction shifted to the family, which fixed and shaped ethical values and convictions.

Because of further fragmentation in the twentieth century, the family is no longer a binding unit for ethics and belief. This function has been taken over by the individual. The whole process of individualism appears to run parallel with the process of secularization. In the very secular twentieth century, every man and woman must choose their own creed and body of ethics. All the collectives have fallen apart, which is not an entirely negative development. In many ways it fits the biblical concept of religion, in which one is a Christian, not by belonging to a certain society, but by personally choosing to believe in and follow Christ.

The second cultural development which has deepened the problem for Christian Ethics is modern relativism. This is far less welcome than individualism. Relativism in morals leads to a rejection of the idea of Natural Law (a body of demands and standards which are built into the very structure of human life and community), and leads to the claim that all morality is merely a matter of social convention. Concepts of good and evil shift according to each person's private likes and preferences. Most people today are moral relativists: They believe that ethics is subject to human choice and manipulation. There is a grain of truth here. There is a field within ethics—the field of customs and habits and conventions—which is historically relative.

But this is not the whole truth. Ethics has been formed from a body of eternal standards: the Decalogue, or Ten Commandments, which do not change. The Ten Commandments are really the most comprehensive rendering of the concept of Natural Law. They consist of demands which life itself makes. One cannot break any of them without hurting oneself or others. They will never become obsolete.

The Decalogue is the bedrock of ethics. Relativism must not erode this. All people acknowledge that there are non-essential, non-ethical areas of life - whether or not, for example, one chooses brown or white toast for breakfast, or a red or green tie to wear to work. The technical term for these non-essentials is *adiaphora*. The relativist wants to make all areas of human act and decision *adiaphora*. The Christian must make distinctions between *adiaphora* and *diaphora*, between the non-essential and the essential (cf. Rom. 2:18). But the essentials should never be allowed to yield to relativism. They must be held firm.

Although relativism is widespread, there is a curious counter-movement to be found in our culture. On the one hand we demand complete freedom concerning personal behaviour. And yet on the other hand, a strong moralism prevails in the public realm, especially in international politics. There is a sharp discrepancy between public and private morality: People have high standards by which they judge, and often denounce, the decisions and actions of public figures, but they consider themselves exempt from these same standards. Only a few people have had the courage to say that this discrepancy does not work. We see today many clamouring public-square moralists, but often these same people are wolves in the board room and libertines in the bedroom. At any rate, people are more aware of moral questions today than they were fifty or one hundred years ago — perhaps because there is so much uncertainty about morality and ethics. Merely open a newspaper, moral questions soak through almost every headline.

3. The Place of Ethics in Theology

Traditionally theology is divided into five disciplines:

- *Old Testament* (introduction to the various books, exegesis, theology, history of Israel);
- *New Testament* (introduction, exegesis, theology, history of New Testament times or background);
- *Church History* (ancient Church, middle ages, reformation, post-reformation, nineteenth to twentieth Century). There exists some debate over the precise division of disciplines between the church historian and the systematician. This involves especially the place of historical theology. It is placed usually within systematic theology.
- *Systematic Theology* is usually divided into dogmatics (what is to be believed, the *credenda*) and ethics (what is to be done, the *agenda*). Systematic theology also usually looks after the field of philosophy of religion and apologetics.
- *Practical Theology* includes homiletics, counselling, liturgical studies, hymnology, and catechetics/Christian education.

Ethics has further been divided into two subcategories: *formal ethics* and *material ethics*. *Formal ethics* answers the question Why? (the reasons, the motives, for action) and Who? (the agent of action). It involves questions concerning conscience, duty, virtue, commands, and natural law. It discusses the language, the categories and the concepts of ethics. *Material ethics* discusses the content and norms of ethics, as well as actual individual moral problem areas, such as the Christian understanding of property holding or the Christian view of marriage.

A third area of ethics concerns basic presuppositions. This is called *Meta-Ethics*, and a proper discussion of it would entail a deep excursion into systematic theology, with references to anthropology, soteriology, and much more. We will not attempt such a vast and ambitious task here.

Introduction to the Decalogue

A. The Decalogue in the Bible

"Decalogue" is a term taken from the Septuagint (LXX), the Greek translation of the Hebrew Bible. It means the "ten words" (Ex. 34:28; Dt. 4:13). The Decalogue is found in Exodus 20:2-17 and Deuteronomy 5:6-21.

1. Institution

The Ten Commandments are a defined body of law for Israel. They are the basic statutes of the Old Covenant. Covenant and Decalogue are closely linked with each other. Exodus 34:28 actually speaks of the "words of the covenant, the Ten Commandments." The Decalogue is even identified as the very content of God's covenant with Israel (Dt. 9:11,15). In Deuteronomy 4:13 the covenant and the Ten Commandments are synonymous.

The two tables of the law were written by the finger of God (Ex. 31:18), and they were deposited in the ark of the covenant (Dt. 10:5). In 2 Chronicles 6:11, Solomon says that the covenant is in the ark (see also Ex. 25:21). 2 Chronicles 5:10 says that the tablets are in the ark, where Aaron's rod and a jar with an omer of manna were also placed (Ex. 36:38; Heb. 9:4).

The Ten Commandments derive their unique authority from their origin. They do not come from man nor through the mediation of man, but from God directly (Ex. 20:1). All other Old Testament laws were mediated through Moses.

2. The Function of the Decalogue in the Old Testament

Although Exodus 20 and Deuteronomy 4 contain the fullest versions of the Decalogue, there are restatements or summaries of it elsewhere in the Old Testament. In his commentary on Exodus, Brevard Childs gives a tripartite summary of the ways in which the Commandments are used : (1) as a lay catechism (the instruction of the people by the Levites); (2) as basic statutes to be proclaimed and renewed at annual feasts (Dt. 31); and (3) as a "confessional mirror" (a technical term from the Middle Ages, referring to little medieval books with lists of sins that "mirrored" the sinfulness of their readers).

(1) The Decalogue comprises a *catechism*. They are the bases for moral instruction. Deuteronomy 4:14 tells us that Moses was to teach the commandments to the people, who in turn were to teach them to their children and grandchildren. Following the deuteronomistic version of the Decalogue there is the famous *Shema Israel*:

"Hear, O Israel: The Lord our God, the Lord is one. Love the Lord your God with all your heart and with all your soul and with all your strength." (Dt. 6:4-5)

This is followed by a statement of God's design for the Decalogue:

"These commandments that I give today are to be upon your hearts. Impress them on your children. Talk about them when you sit at home and when you walk along the road, when you lie down and when you get up. Tie them as symbols on your hands and bind them on your foreheads. Write them on the doorframes of your houses and on your gates." (Dt. 6:6-9)

The Israelites fulfilled this injunction literally: phylacteries, or pieces of leather worn around the forehead or on the left arm, have been found in Qumran which have the *Shema* and sometimes the entire Ten Commandments written on them.

The Decalogue was the heart of the Covenant and they were continually read at synagogue services. In early Israel, they were omnipresent.

(2) The Decalogue is also *legislation:*. The Ten Commandments are spliced together with Israel's oldest criminal code, "The Book of the Covenant" (Ex.21-23), with at least five of the Ten Commandments being repeated within the Book of the Covenant itself (the first and fourth commandments occur in Exodus 23:12-

13, and the fifth, sixth and eighth commandments occur in Exodus 21:12-17). As well, some of the other commandments are repeated in another legal text, in the "holiness code" (Lev. 19), which also incorporates five commandments, the first, fourth, fifth, eighth and ninth.

(3) The Decalogue also has an *accusatory* function: it is used in prophetic accusation of the sinner (Jer. 7:6-9; Hos. 4:2; Ez. 22:6; Ps. 50: 18-20). The first two uses of the Decalogue, its catechetical and legislative functions, are designed for shaping and informing human action. They come before the deed. The accusatory function, however, comes after the deed. Its design is to reform human action. The Ten Commandments stood at the centre of Old Testament ethics and were the touchstones for judging all deeds. They were the basis for all moral and legal accusation.

These three categories of usage—catechism, legislation, and accusation—are important, for they comprise the three uses of the Law in Protestant ethics as well.

3. The Reaffirmation and Interpretation of the Decalogue in the New Testament

The New Testament also includes clusters of the Ten Commandments, although all ten do not occur in any one place. They are taken for granted throughout the New Testament.

(1) A group of commandments is found in The Sermon on the Mount (Mt. 5-7). The Sermon on the Mount is not, as some have claimed, a rescinding of the Decalogue. In those passages where Christ says, "You have heard it said ... but I say to you," although he appears to be setting his own teaching over against that of the Old Testament law, he is in fact only using this antithetical form for the sake of emphasis. He is not supplanting the Commandments, but radicalizing them. He adds, or rather restores, to the commandments the element of intention: to commit an act—murder or adultery, for example—in one's heart is as corrupting and ultimately as blameworthy as committing it in deed.

The sixth commandment, not to kill, is repeated in Mt. 5:21. The seventh commandment, not to commit adultery, is repeated in Mt. 5:27. Christ's admonition against the swearing of oaths (Mt. 5:33-37) is a radicalization of the third and ninth commandments, that is, not to take the Lord's name in vain and not to bear false witness.

It is difficult to distinguish precisely the nature of Christ's use of the Ten Commandments in the Sermon on the Mount. Is he providing catechetical material or an interpretation of the law (he, after all, includes penalties for disobedience)? Or is the Sermon on the Mount a genre of legislation?

(2) In Matthew 15:4-6, individual commandments are quoted verbatim. Jesus juxtaposes the word of God and human traditions. He denounces the habit of interpreting the law in such a way that they are, in effect, nullified.

(3) Matthew 15:19 has a rather full list of the commandments (the sixth, the seventh twice, the eight, the ninth, and the third). Christ uses here a kind of short hand; he names a litany of offenses, "evil thoughts, murder, adultery, sexual immorality, theft, false testimony, slander", which the corresponding Commandments sternly prohibit. Again, it is not entirely clear what the genre is here. Is it an interpretation of the law or a prophetic accusation of the sinner? In this case, it is probably the latter.

(4) A fairly full treatment is found in Matthew 19, where the sixth, seventh, eighth, ninth, and fifth as well as the commandment to "Love your neighbour" (Lev. 19:18) are touched on. "If you would enter life," Christ says, "keep these commandments." The exhortation is reminiscent of Psalms 15 and 24, the "temple entrance liturgies." The context for these commandments is *a priori*, before the deed.

(5) In Romans 13:9 Paul quotes the seventh, sixth, eighth and tenth Commandments verbatim, and summarizes the rest with the cursory phrase "and whatever other commandments there might be." The context here is a generalization of ethical duties, and Paul, like Christ, sums all of the commandments up with the injunction to "love your neighbour as yourself." Love is the rubric and touchstone of the Ten Commandments. It subsumes the Decalogue. The Greek term for "sum up" (*anakefalaioutai*) refers here both to "recapitulation" and "comprehension"; love is not the reduction of the Ten Commandments, their lowest common denominator, but the fullness of them (cf. Jas. 2:8). Love is the head and the Ten Commandments are the members. They are subordinate, and yet the body cannot be reduced to the head. The Ten Commandments are the substructure of Christian ethics, of which the edifice is love. The Ten Commandments are the exposition of the central commandment to love. They are the predicates of love.

(6) In 1 Timothy 1: 8-10 the sixth, seventh, eighth, and ninth commandments are cited in an open-ended list similar to Romans 13:9. Paul addresses as well the question of how to interpret the Law Christianly, the hermeneutics of the Decalogue. "We know that the law is good if one uses it properly," that is, according to its designed use. Again, the goal of the Commandments, we are told, is love (1 Tim. 1:5). But the law is also "made not for the righteous but for lawbreakers and rebels, the ungodly and sinful, the unholy and irreligious" (1:9). Correct application, then, is paramount: to the godly, it is a guide to love; to the sinner, it is goad to repentance; to the miscreant, it is the basis of their guiltiness before God and man.

So the New Testament includes six places where clusters of the Commandments are quoted. Three passages are fundamental restatements. The other three passages use, apparently, the same three categories—legislation, accusation, and catechism—which we delineated in the Old Testament. 1 Timothy 1:9,10 emphasises the Law's function of restraining the evildoer. This passage has a legal ring to it. Matthew 15:19 is in the style of prophetic accusation, a general indictment against the human heart. And Romans 13:8-10, where Paul speaks of the Ten Commandments as an exposition of the command to love, serves as a kind of catechetical guideline for the life of the believer.

B. The Decalogue in the History of the Teaching of the Church

1. The First Two Centuries

Many early Christian writers knew and quoted individual commandments. They were freely interspersed with other ethical material, often presented in the scheme of the "two ways": the good way and the evil way. The golden rule (Mt. 7:12) was often given as the overall rationale for the Commandments. Discussions of the Commandments are found in the *Didache* (second Century), the *Shepherd of Hermas*, and the *Letter of Barnabas*. They always include due application of the Commandments to new problems which Christians encountered within Greek culture. For example, the command not to kill was expanded to abortion and infanticide, crimes which were not found in Israel.

Bishop Irenaeus (ca. 180) reaffirmed the Commandments in his battle against Marcionite antinomianism. Irenaeus contended that the Commandments were not, as the Marcionites claimed, abrogated by the New Covenant. He argues that Christ has not abolished the Commandments but rather empowered us to keep them, for "unless your righteousness surpasses that of the Pharisees and the teachers of the law, you will certainly not enter the kingdom of heaven" (Mt. 5:20). Irenaeus was the first to consciously associate the Ten Commandments with the Greek concept of natural law (a law which God has "written on the hearts of all people, which they can know and understand through mere reason.")

Paul speaks of such a phenomenon in Romans 2:14-15. Even if the heathen have not received divine revelation, if God has not specifically unveiled His will to them, they nevertheless have been given knowledge through their consciences of God's moral standards. Irenaeus, then, identifies the Ten Commandments with Natural Law, and argues that Christ, in the Sermon on the Mount, extends this basic body of morality to include a specifically Christian dimension. But the fundamental Commandments remain the same in both Testaments.

2. The Church Fathers

The status of the Ten Commandments deteriorated during the time of the Church fathers. Clement of Alexandria (d. 215) held them in high esteem, but his pupil Origen (185-254) began the process that, like water and wind on hard rock, eroded the importance of these Commandments once chiselled in stone. Origen viewed the Ten Commandments as a primitive law unable to compete with elaborate, sophisticated pagan Greek moral teaching. Shortly after him, Jerome (350-420), in the same vein, spoke of them as milk for infants but not sufficient as food for moral athletes. This devaluation of the Ten Commandments was largely due to the corresponding construction, and exaltation, of the ethics of the "Counsels of Perfection," whereby on the basis of Matthew 19:11 and 21, celibacy and poverty came to be seen as the higher or superior calling for a Christian. These "Counsels of Perfection" were set over against the Ten Commandments, as something superseding them.

Augustine (354-430) held that the Ten Commandments were a pre-Christian law and thought of the double commandment of love as Christ's ingenious simplification of ethics. Augustine stressed that the Christian is not steered from the outside by a law on two tablets, but is rather moved from the inside "because God has poured out his love into our hearts" (Rom. 5:5). Goodness is not exacted from the Christian, but wells up from within him. Contextualization was a problem for Augustine, as it is today. In his surroundings, he felt that in doing ethics one needed to describe a positive ethical aim. A stark list of "do not's" was insufficient for the Greek moralist, who sought perfection of character. The Greeks scorned a mere minimum ethics, which the Ten Commandments appeared to be, and cherished the projection of an ideal character. Thus, Augustine promoted the positive commandment of love as the Christian moral ideal.

But it was St. Ambrose (339-397), Augustine's teacher, who really determined the next 800 years of Christian ethics. Ambrose wrote the first textbook on Christian ethics, *On the Duties of the Clerics (De officiis ministrorum)*, modelled after Cicero's *On the Duties (De officiis)*. He replaced the Ten Commandments with an ethical structure built around the four Greek cardinal virtues: Justice, Prudence, Fortitude and Temperance. He believed that he was able to discern these same virtues in the Bible. (Wisdom 8:7, which is part of the Apocrypha, lists these exact four virtues, which is due to Greek philosophical influence during inter-testamental times). Ambrose added to these four the Christian virtues of Faith, Hope and Love. And these four philosophical and three theological virtues determined the shape and content of Christian ethics for the next 800 years.

The medieval ethical system mingled the commandments with the Counsels of Perfection. Irenaeus had spoken of the two levels of ethics: The Old Testament with the Ten Commandments (Natural Law), and the Sermon on the Mount. The Sermon on the Mount was "surpassing righteousness" (Mt. 5:20). Ambrose and Jerome developed further this two-level structure, which resembles closely the Stoic moral scheme. It had also two levels: "duty" and "perfect action" (perfect, that is, with a view to the moral destiny of man). "Duty" comprises all those actions which nature demands of us if we are to sustain our creational life, the proper or fitting actions. Sometimes these are called "middle" actions, between failure (sin) and perfection. Beyond the middle actions are the perfect actions, those acts that not only sustain us but better us.

The New Testament was divided up according to these distinctions. So the Ten Commandments became the "duty", at the lower level, and the Sermon on the Mount embodied the ideal of perfection: to love your enemy, to pray for those who persecute you, to bless those who curse you - such things exceed the demands of nature. They are the protocol of perfection. Jerome thought that Paul makes a similar distinction between what is required and what is best in his discussion on the virgins in 1 Corinthians 7. Paul says he has no "commandment" from the Lord, and yet he gives "counsel." In the Vulgate, Jerome's translation of the Bible into common, "vulgar" Latin, Jerome sees this distinction between commandment and counsel as corresponding to the two-level ethical structure of duties and perfection. He sees, as well, the same two-level scheme underlying Christ's response to the rich young ruler in Matthew 19:16-22. The rich young ruler, seeking perfection, is first pointed to the Ten Commandments. Only after he claims to have satisfied these does Christ point him to perfection, "If you want to be perfect," is Christ's phrase, and then tells him to give away all his possessions. So, for the Church Fathers, perfection involved voluntary poverty (Mt. 19), virginity or continence (1 Cor. 7), and a vow of obedience to a superior: the monastic ideal as the ethics of the Counsels of Perfection. The Church Fathers, then, reduced the Ten Commandments from a primer for the masses to the handbook of the few. From the time of Ambrose, perfection was a priviledge reserved for the few. Perfection was only for Jerome's "athletes," the monks and nuns.

A third element helped to reduce the importance of the Decalogue during the Middle Ages. This was the attempt to describe the Christian way of life in a positive way with a small and simplified number of catechetical applications, like the eight beatitudes (Mt. 5), or the seven physical works of mercy (Mt. 25:31-36). To this was added from Tobit 2:9, which is part of the Apocrypha, the sacred duty to bury the dead.

This list was later complemented with the seven spiritual works of mercy: to counsel, to rebuke when necessary, to teach, to comfort, to forgive, to suffer the other, and to pray for one's neighbour. Another list was made up of the seven gifts of the Spirit, understood as seven virtues (Isa. 11:2): wisdom, understanding, counsel, fortitude, knowledge and the fear of the Lord (a word in the Vulgate from the verse that follows was added to make seven).

Thus, the Middle Ages produced various moral lists which, rather than supplementing, supplanted the Ten Commandments. In defence of these lists, we must note that they are comprised of biblical material, not just gleanings from pagan culture. But, nevertheless, their effect was to eclipse the Decalogue in the Middle Ages.

To these several lists of moral virtues we might add some of the representative lists of sins which the Middle Age also produced. There were lists of the sins of the five senses, a number of crying sins, a number of mute sins, and a list of the sins of the various situations in life. The representative list, of course, is that of the seven deadly sins. Together, these lists of virtues and sins replaced the Ten Commandments during the period of approximately 400-1200.

3. The Recovery of the Decalogue during the Middle Ages

A popular myth in Protestant circles says that the Reformation alone restored the Ten Commandments. But this is not true historically. A recovery began in the thirteenth century. Even though negative morality, the thundering Thou Shalt Nots of the Ten Commandments, was scorned as catechetical and apologetic material, there was one area of church life in which a negatively coded morality was highly appropriate. This was the institution of Penance. The Ten Commandments were used here as a confessional mirror. Each commandment was broken down into a certain number of sins in casuistic fashion so that the confessor could see on a list the penance required for specific sins. This practice, along with the description of the Ten Commandments as the confessional mirror of the church, was introduced in Britain through a book by Edmund of Canterbury (d. 1246). Bonaventura (1221-1274), the great Franciscan, gave a full exposition of the Decalogue. Even Bernard of Clairvaux (1090-1153) a hundred years earlier wrote an exposition of the Ten Commandments (the authorship of this particular work is disputed, however).

By the thirteenth century the Ten Commandments were again at the heart of the Church. This great reversal is evident in Thomas Aquinas (1224-1274), the greatest of the Scholastics, who discusses most of the Ten Commandments individually in his *Summa Theologiae*. He used, however, the Greek virtues for the structure of his ethics. But in the last year of his life, he gave a series of sermons for laity and fellow Dominicans on the Ten Commandments. The fourteenth and fifteenth centuries were dominated by the Decalogue, mostly in their negative function as a list of sins.

4. The Decalogue in the Reformation (Luther & Calvin)

There was both discontinuity and continuity in the view of the Decalogue in the Reformation. It abolished the two-level ethics, where Counsels of Perfection were placed above the Decalogue. But on the other hand the Reformation continued and developed the usage of the Ten Commandments for both confession and catechism. Martin Luther and his colleagues categorically attacked the two-level scheme in which the second level was the touchstone of perfection and involved excess merit and reward. In his attack on monasticism he did away with them, by reinterpreting the New Testament. He spiritualized them: Every Christian is asked by Christ to live free of the grip of possessions and of lust and in obedience to superiors. No Christian is exempt from those three vows. In addition, the other demands taken from the Sermon on the Mount (love for one's enemies, intercessory prayer for those who persecute you) are demanded from every Christian. They are not *ad libitum* ("at pleasure"), but Christian duty.

Thus, Luther distils the whole of Christian ethics into the Ten Commandments. But he expounds them with such fullness that they embrace all New Testament exhortation. Luther abolishes the medieval distinction between two groups of Christians. He shows that the Ten Commandments contain all that is demanded of every Christian. Luther said repeatedly that if we really love God with all our heart and mind and soul and strength, then we will be fully occupied and need not seek after some higher form of piety or merit.

The Reformation positively continued the medieval tradition of using the Ten Commandments for confession manuals and general catechism for the broad masses. Luther wrote fifteen different printed expositions of the Ten Commandments. The first was a series of sermons published in 1516 in Wittenburg. At the same time he prepared a small instruction manual which, for the purpose of leading the reader to confession, used the Ten Commandments as a mirror for examining the conscience. The suggestion at the end of Luther's *Small Catechism* is, still, that the Ten Commandments should be used as a confessional mirror. In that work, the section on ethics is made up exclusively of an exposition of the Ten Commandments and a list of the order of vocations in life. Together, these two things comprise the whole body of ethics in Reformational teaching. Luther's high esteem for the Decalogue is expressed in his *Large Catechism*:

> "Here then we have the Ten Commandments as a divine summary of what we are to do to make our whole life pleasing to God. They are the true fountain from which all good works must spring. They are the true channel through which all good works must flow. Apart from these Ten Commandments no deed, no conduct can be pleasing to God, no matter how great and precious it may be in the eyes of the world." (The Book of Concord, ed. Th. Tappert, Fortress 1959, p. 407)

Luther said that we should have the Ten Commandments always before our eyes, engrafted on our memories, so that, in whatever situation we find ourselves, we immediately think about what our deeds and decisions mean in terms of the Ten Commandments. Clearly, then, he believed that the Ten Commandments provided a sufficient situational ethic. That is why he concludes,

> *"From all this it is obvious how highly these Ten Commandments are to be exalted and extolled above all orders, commands and works which are taught and practised apart from them.... Therefore we should prize and value them above all other teachings as the greatest treasure God has given us."* (Idem, p. 410)

This is Luther, but his voice is that of the whole Protestant Reformation.

Calvin, in the first chapter of the first edition (1536) of his *Institutes,* gave an exposition of the Ten Commandments. For Calvin, 'Law' means the Ten Commandments. Following Luther, he teaches that the Law comes before the Gospel, as a means of preparation for accepting the Gospel. His echoing of Luther is due to the fact that at this stage Calvin follows the structure of Luther's Catechisms: the Ten Commandments, the apostolic creeds and, only then, the Lord's Prayer.

The Ten Commandments are also central to Calvin's *Catechism* (Geneva, 1536). This has fifty-eight sections, fourteen of which (sections eight to twenty-one) are on the Law as steps to Christ. In ten of these sections (nine to eighteen), Calvin considers the Ten Commandments individually. So, when Calvin speaks of ethics, he speaks of the Ten Commandments. The same is true of his famous major catechism, the *Geneva Catechism* (Geneva, in French 1541, and in Latin 1545). It asks and answers 373 questions. Law, treated in questions 131-232, is discussed only after faith. Calvin emphasizes two functions of the Law: its accusing work and its guiding work. He sees the Ten Commandments as the rule for the life of the believer, the "perfect rule of righteousness." This catechism was used each Sunday, at twelve noon, with young people aged ten to fifteen. They had to recite, in similar fashion to the Lutheran churches of that time, the *Catechism* before they were admitted to holy communion. In 1561 this practice became part of the church constitution and, with it, the *Geneva Catechism* became the basis for ordaining the clergy. In this manner, the Ten Commandments were incorporated in a Reformation confessional document. Calvin also referred to the Decalogue extensively in his commentaries and sermons.

For the Reformers, then, the Decalogue is in content identical with Natural Law. Because man's perception of God's commandments, the Natural Law, had been skewed and blurred by his fallenness, the Reformers taught that man needs fresh revelation of those commandments, and was given this in the Decalogue. The Decalogue is the law of God. The Christian's task is to fulfil the Law, for it is the content of Christian ethics. What Christ brought is not a new law or an abolition of the old law, but rather a new power to keep the commandments. Christ provides new motivation, but no new ethic. The Reformers spoke, then, of the New Testament as an implementation but not an extension of the Old Testament ethical material, against Irenaeus and the tradition which hails from him.

In the centuries that followed, the Ten Commandments were reaffirmed and defended, beginning with the theological battles of the sixteenth century. In time, it became the standard code of ethics in all Protestant orthodoxy. Christian ethics, therefore, was equated, often with elaborate exposition, with the Ten Commandments for several centuries. Christian ethics *is* the Ten Commandments.

5. Modernity

What, then, has been the status of the Ten Commandments in the teaching of the Church over the past two centuries? Their glory has, in a word, faded. Modern times are characterized by the defection of ethics from the Ten Commandments. This defection began at the beginning of the nineteenth century with Friedrich Schleiermacher (1768-1834), the great grandfather of all modern liberal theology. In his famous book *The Christian Faith*, he declared the Decalogue inappropriate as catechetical material because it gives a wrong impression of the Christian life, as if it consisted in merely keeping commandments. Schleiermacher set the tone that pervades the nineteenth century.

In the second half of the century, Albrecht Ritschl (1822-1889), the grandfather of liberalism, restored with great force the reformational ethics of vocation. He made the concept of vocation central, not only to ethics, but also to Christology. Christ's greatness, he taught, was rooted in his devotion to his calling. Ritschl, though, is conspicuously silent about the Decalogue. These towering figures in theology have determined much of the attitude in the twentieth century.

The first textbook in ethics, following the renewal of theology in the 1920's by Karl Barth's dialectical theology inspired largely by Soren Kierkegaard, was Emil Brunner's *The Divine Imperative* (1932). It contains not a single section nor a paragraph on the Ten Commandments. It is as if they do no exist.

The twentieth century, because of its mood of lawlessness, has not been favourable to the reformational retention of the Ten Commandments. We exalt liberty to the extent that we eclipse responsibility, and in so doing we come close to that heresy of the early church; namely antinomianism. The Ten Commandments are, especially outside the church, under heavy fire. They have been shucked like corn husks. In 1980, the U.S. Supreme Court ruled in effect that it was unconstitutional to display the Ten Commandments in a public classroom—a biting irony, since the Ten Commandments are painted on the walls of the Supreme Court.

This modern hostility towards the Decalogue has suffused the Church. Part of this is due to a widespread feeling among Christians that the Ten Commandments are, like a glass vial, too narrow and brittle a rule for life. They want something more. And they wonder that if all ethics are summed up in the Decalogue, where then does the New Testament fit into the plan for Christian living. Are Christians, they ask, distinguished from Jews only by dogmatics and not at all by ethics? What, then, happens to the enormous amount of New Testament ethical material? So there is, as we saw in our survey of the Middle Ages, a search in the twentieth century for a specifically Christian ethics.

What this search gave birth to is the so-called "new morality" movement of the 1960s. Its slogan was "situational ethics" : We must, in each situation, decide what is right for ourselves in that situation. Ethical decisions, in effect, cannot be made prior to or independent of any given situation. Such an ethics dispenses with absolutes, and so discards the Ten Commandments. There is only one commandment this ethics recognizes, one principle it acknowledges: The commandment of love. Joseph Fletcher, a representative of situational ethics in America, has only scorn for the Ten Commandments. In Britain his colleague Bishop J. A. T. Robinson of London thought that, in modern technological society, they were only a nuisance.

But this is not a liberal problem only. Among some conservatives there is a dismissiveness or even outright hostility toward the Ten Commandments. A certain strata of Dispensationalists, for example, claim that the Ten Commandments belong to an obsolete dispensation that has nothing to do with Christians. By this they do not mean, of course, that Christians are free to trespass against the moral content of the Commandments. But they feel that the format is theologically outdated.

So, the extreme right and the extreme left meet in their suspicion of the Ten Commandments.

C. The Hermeneutics of the Decalogue

1. Method of Exposition

Calvin's *Institutes* comprise the first Systematic Theology of the Reformation. Before Calvin goes into detailed exposition, he first discusses his methodology (*Institutes* II, 8, 8). Calvin says that God means to teach us more than just the naked words of the Decalogue. We must, he says, in exposition of the Decalogue, do the following: 1) find the meaning of the specific commandment; 2) find the purpose of the divine legislator: What pleases or displeases Him? 3) find the opposite of the commandment. The clear assumption behind 3 is that, if the Lord forbids one thing, he commands its opposite. This is Calvin's "Rule of Opposites." Virtue, then, is, not merely the avoidance of wrong, but the performance of the good. "You shall not murder" (Ex. 20:13) means both what it says as well as what it implies: "You shall preserve life, protect it." Both are commanded.

In *Institutes* II, 8, 8, Calvin crafts the shortest statement of this principle: "If this [the content of the Commandment] pleases God, the opposite displeases him." Proscriptions imply prescriptions! This method of exposition is called *synecdoche* (II, 8, 8; II, 8, 10), which means a figure of speech where one part (the crown) may stand for the whole (the monarchy). Another case of *synecdoche* is where a cause stands for its effect, or vice versa.

Johannes Wollebius in his *Compendium Theologiae Christianae* (1626) echoes Calvin. In every specific instance the entire picture must be kept in mind. This is the secret behind the Reformational belief that the Ten Commandments sufficiently describe and subsume the whole of Christian ethics. The Ten Commandments have tucked within them hidden dimensions, rich and vast, which are opened up by the method of *synecdoche*. Calvin's methodological discovery, like the discovery that an old, dented, rust-scabbed trunk contained, once pried open, a hoard of jewels, created a new fervour for the Ten Commandments. This explains the proliferation of expositions on the Ten Commandments which came in its wake.

Some of these expositions degenerated into massive casuistry. For example, in England, sleeping during church was treated as a violation of the Third Commandment, "You shall not misuse the name of the LORD your God." In this, *synecdoche* became a cul-de-sac. And yet we need to be open, though cautious, to the usefulness of this method.

An exposition of the Great Commission by way of *synecdoche* illustrates the limits of this method. God calls some people to leave their civil vocation and enter into cross-cultural evangelism. We might delineate such a call as part of the general duty of witnessing and then, by *synecdoche*, extrapolate this principle into the positive equivalent of not using the Lord's name in vain. But this is not satisfactory. For not everyone is called to cross-cultural evangelism. This is the weakness of casuistry: It can describe different situations but it cannot anticipate the calling of an individual. The method of *synecdoche* is useful, and we will use it, but we must not pretend that it encompasses the whole of Christian ethics.

Let us begin by doing basic Christian ethics. We will look at both the prohibition and, by *synecdoche*, the positive counterpart. We will interpret the Ten Commandments mainly from the Bible itself. The material here is mostly negative: a kind of land-clearing enterprise, where the stumps and roots of human sinfulness are cleared away to make room for civilized life. Sin must be uprooted before virtue is planted.

The New Testament gives mostly a positive restatement of the Ten Commandments. This is the particular contribution of New Testament teaching. For example, the so-called Golden Rule (Mt. 7:12) can be found in Greek and pre-Christian rabbinic writings. But it is usually stated in its negative form: do not do to others what you do not want done to you. As a formula, this distils the ethic of avoidance—the teaching that virtue consists in what you do not do rather than in what you do, in what evil you sidestep rather than in what good you promote. Virtue is keeping your white robes unsullied. The New Testament turns this around. Christ preaches an ethic of involvement, not withdrawal, of pursuing the good, not just avoiding the bad. This, in essence, pinpoints the difference between Christian and pre-Christian ethics.

So, the pattern of exposition will be as follows: first, the commandment, stated negatively; and then an examination of the positive fulfilment, both in the Old and in the New Testament.

2. Applications of the Decalogue

How do the Ten Commandments function in the lives of those who hear them? This is a question about the offices or uses of the Ten Commandments. Melanchthon in *Loci Communes* (1535), a textbook of dogmatics, outlines three uses, or "duties," of the Decalogue (*Melanchton on Christian Doctrine* (1965) pp. 122-128):

1) *Civil use*. The commandments are incorporated into the law of the land. They work to constrain evil, to hold back the potential criminal;

2) *Accusing use*. The theological technical term is *Usus elenchthicus*, meaning "reprimand, rebuke, accuse, condemn." The second use of the Law, then, is to convict the sinner of their sin (cf. Rom. 3:20). In this use, the Law prepares the way for the Gospel. The logic here is simple: Just as you must first feel your sickness before you are aware of your need for the doctor, so too you must first know your sinfulness before you know your need for the saviour;

3) *Teaching use*. The Ten Commandments, shorn of their curse and condemnation, return to the regenerate believer as ethical instruction, lights by which to steer the life of sanctification.

The Reformers said that whenever the Ten Commandments are preached or taught, some will be prevented from doing evil, some will be convicted and driven to Christ, and some will be taught a practical lesson for daily living. They used three images to illustrate the three uses: a fence—to hem in the good, and keep out the bad; a mirror—to reveal the sinner in his nakedness and neediness; and a ruler—to mark out the standards by which the righteous shall live. Calvin speaks of the commandments even as a bridle and whip for the believer (*Institutes* II, 7, 6-12).

Theologians discuss whether or not Luther had three uses of the Decalogue or only the civil and convicting uses. Some argue that if you hold to these two uses you are soundly Reformational in your ethics but if you add the third you slip towards legalism. Luther never says explicitly that there are three uses. But in *On Good Works*, he gives a positive exposition of each of the Ten Commandments. So, even if in theory Luther never commended the third use, as a Christian's rule for life, in practice he did.

These three uses are deeply rooted in the Scriptures themselves. We saw six restatements of the Ten Commandments in the New Testament. Three are straight quotations, but the other three apply the Ten Commandments in particular ways; each corresponds exactly to the three uses which the Reformers delineated. In 1 Timothy 1:8-10 we see the law used as a restraining force (first use); in Matthew 15:19, we see it operating in its accusing function (second use); and in Romans 13:8-10, we see the law used as the rule for godly living (third use). In Romans 13 Paul does not mean that love supplants the commandments, but that love is exegeted and unfolded by the Ten Commandments. They define the shape and content of love. Christian love is the Ten Commandments tallied.

3. The Place of the Decalogue in a System of Christian Ethics

a) Collecting Materials

Let us gather materials from Scripture for a Christian ethics. From the Old Testament, there are three bodies of material that interest us: moral law; civil (or judicial) law (for example, the Book of the Covenant (Ex. 21-23)); and Ceremonial law (that is laws which have to do with the cult of Israel, for example, the laws of sacrifice). From the New Testament, there is the ethical teaching of Jesus (for example, the Sermon on the Mount), the ethical teaching of the apostles, the exhortation material in the letters (often the second half of the letters), ethical instructions addressed to others (for example, Jesus' words to the rich young ruler (Mt. 19), or the Holy Spirit directing Paul to cross over to Macedonia (Acts 16:6-10)).

b) Examination

Are these materials suitable for Christian ethics? As we have seen, the Ten Commandments have been received into Christian ethics. They are part of a timeless body of ethical instruction for the people of God, past, present and future. They have been validated by Christ and the New Testament as an exposition of the double commandment of love. They can be shown to represent Natural Law, that which is built into the core structure of the moral universe, just as the law of gravity is woven into the texture of physical world. They also shed light on the Golden Rule (Mt. 7:12). From the Old Testament, we want to retain the moral law. But what about the civil and ceremonial laws?

c) The Civil Law

Thomas Aquinas came up with a neat and clear formula for the civil law: When there is a change of statehood there is a change of laws. Israel's civil law does not qualify as ethics for the Christian church simply because the civil state of ancient Israel no longer exists. Therefore, the civil law doesn't apply any longer because it was the civil law of that state. The church is not a nation-state. It does not, therefore, have civil jurisdiction or capital punishment. A law such as the one found in Exodus 21:2, "If you buy a Hebrew servant, he is to serve you for six years," is irrelevant in a society without slaves. Similarly, a law such as that contained in Exodus 21:17, "Anyone who curses his father or mother must be put to death," prescribes a penalty which is no longer applicable. Such laws exist only as a function of the state that supports and enforces them. When the state collapses, the laws do too.

But the reformers taught that it is wise and useful to draw on Israel's ordinances for one's individual moral life or as suggestions for legislation in the state in which one lives. Some ordinances are eminently applicable under changed circumstances, for example, "do not mistreat an alien or oppress him, ..." (Ex. 22:21). We were never sojourners in Egypt, but the material does not thereby cease to inspire moral vision; it tells us what is right in the eyes of God.

Regardless of the moral fruitfulness of such ordinances, they cannot be made mandatory as a body. Johannes Wollebius stated the final formula of the reformed orthodox fathers:

> "On those matters on which it is in harmony with moral law and ordinary justice, it [the civil law of Israel] is binding. Of those matters which were peculiar to that law and which were prescribed for the promised land or the Jewish state has no more force for us than the laws of other foreign commonwealths. So we heed only those elements of the civil law which are compatible with our situation and the original moral law."

d) The Ceremonial Law

The ceremonial law of Israel has been abrogated in the Christian church. Israel's cult of sacrifice has been replaced by Christ himself [Christ as the high priest (Heb. 4:14) and Christ as the sacrificial lamb (1 Cor. 5:7)]. Calvin points out (*Institutes* II, 7, 16) that the only present value of the ceremonial law is as interpretive material for Christology. Thomas Aquinas makes the distinction clear. He said that these laws are not only dead but deadly, to continue to practice them is to ignore the once-for-all sacrifice made by Christ (see Heb. 10:1-14).

e) *The New Testament Material*

The exhortational material is certainly binding for all Christians (see, for example, Eph. 4-6). But we have to make some distinctions, to separate out the instructions Jesus gave specifically to individuals. For example, the command to the rich young ruler cannot be generalized in Christian ethics. There were other disciples who were not commanded to sell all (see, for example: Luke 8:3, about the wealthy women who share their possessions with the disciples; Luke 19, about rich Zacheus; Acts 12:12, about Mary, the mother of John Mark, who owns a house). The Holy Spirit's directives given in the train of the missionary advance of the early church included very detailed instruction *to individuals*. They were given to individual people at a certain time in a certain place. This is the triadic formula for situational ethics: individual time, individual place, individual person. These individual instructions cannot become part of the general body of ethics. The reformers saw this with particular clarity. They said that, if we did not winnow out the individual from the universal, the specific from the general, we would end in building another ark. Simply put, not all of the New Testament's individual instructions can be generalized. But we do well to remember that the category of individual instruction exists: Jesus and, in His stead, the Holy Spirit, can and does give individuals specific guidance for a particular time and a particular place.

Christian ethics includes the Ten Commandments, with their compatible material in the Prophets and the wisdom literature, as well as the New Testament parenetical material (both in the gospels and the letters), and the principle of individual direction given by Jesus and the Holy Spirit.

f) *A Systematization of the Materials*

What is the place of the Decalogue in a system of Christian ethics? A fruitful image for describing Christian ethics is a wedding cake. The bottom layer of the cake is creation ethics, the creation ordinances, which include the cultural commission and procreation commission from Genesis. This level includes all the materials necessary for the preservation of life and community. Such materials make up the God-given user's manual for creation and procreation, for living on earth and in community. They instruct us in creational stewardship and human companionship, and so include the Golden Rule (Mt. 7:12), the Decalogue (as consonant with Natural Law), and the summary of the Decalogue in the double commandment of love. All these things are necessary for the healthy continuation of the human race and the individual.

To put it another way, this is an ethics of preservation. A surprising amount of New Testament material falls into this category. The six works of mercy (Mt. 25:34-46), for example, which are the standard of divine judgement, are acts of sustenance, of meeting human need. And elsewhere (Mk. 3:4), Jesus identifies saving life with doing good. This ethics of preservation forms the basis of social ethics and civil law. Its commandments—to feed, to clothe, to protect—are not distinctively Christian: they are intelligible to and therefore mandatory for all people. They are the common basis for structuring life, especially today in a pluralistic society. We can derive from them social, medical and legal ethics.

Thus, the first layer of our "wedding cake" is distributed to all and not just to the wedding party. It is not distinctly Christian, but nevertheless foundational to Christian ethics.

The second layer of our "cake" is comprised of material not shared by other religions or cultures. This is not the ethics of creation or of humankind, but the ethics of salvation for believers. Here faith is presupposed. This layer includes the following: the New Testament exhortation material directed toward both shaping individual Christian character and communal life within the church; the love, exceeding the demands of the Golden Rule, for one's enemies; the waiving of the right to civil justice (1 Cor. 6); and the Great Commission.

This same two-level ethics is evident in Calvin's *Institutes*. He speaks first of the Decalogue and then of the Christian life. There is a body of ethics before and after conversion. This, however, is different from the distinction made in the Middle Ages. In the Protestant ethical structure, there is no scheme of merit attached. As well, the two-levelled ethics distinguishes not two separate groups of Christians—the rabble and the righteous—but rather two different stages in the life of an individual.

Is this a valid distinction? Suspicion is justified. For example, does the story of the good Samaritan (Lk. 10:30-37) portray distinctly Christian behaviour? Perhaps it does, but, it equally portrays the preservation, succour and sustenance of creation.

What, then, is the relation of the second level to the first? Perhaps the second level is only a duplication of the first, but with more power? If the first level speaks of tending life, like a gardener, the second level speaks of saving life, like a doctor. The Pharisees were content with being good, religious, and healthy. Jesus was concerned with doing good, practising religion, and restoring health. The first level is designed to preserve the good, the second, to bring it about.

The third layer on our "cake" encompasses divine instruction to individuals in a particular time and place. An example of this is when Peter was sent to Cornelius (Acts 10:19). Another example is when individuals are sometimes called to waive their natural rights, such as the creational right to a home and family and property, especially in the case of foreign mission and extraordinary domestic charity. These individual instructions, though they do not contradict or violate the other two levels of ethics but are rather supported by them, cannot be directly inferred from those two levels.

What we have, then, is a three-fold ethics that can be thought of as trinitarian in shape. The Father corresponds to creational ethics, the Son to redemption ethics, and the Holy Spirit to the ethics of individual guidance.

This is basic Christian ethics. It is an ethics with two taproots: Scripture and Spirit. Both must be held together, because if one eclipses the other, ethics either hardens into legalism or unravels into antinomianism. The Decalogue must be defended against lawlessness, both in society and as a theological principle; and yet the Decalogue must not be made as stony and cold as the rock it was carved in, but must remain supple so that it can be extended both to the New Testament material and to the individual instruction of the Holy Spirit. Christian ethics must hold a third position between lawlessness and legalism.

4. Appendix on the Counting of the Commandments

There are two different ways of counting the Ten Commandments. The Lutheran and the Roman Catholic way has three commandments on the first table (concerning God) and seven on the second table (concerning one's neighbour). This way rolls into one commandment the misuse of God's name and the prohibition against making idols. They treat the prohibition against images as the same thing as the prohibition against having other gods—a position which has some grounds linguistically and theologically, for both image-making and the worship of other gods are idolatry. In order to derive Ten Commandments, then, the Lutherans and Roman Catholics divide the Tenth Commandment into two commandments. "You shall not covet your neighbour's house" is the Ninth Commandment, and "You shall not covet your neighbour's wife ..." is the Tenth. The Orthodox and Reformed way has four on the first table and six on the second.

THE FIRST COMMANDMENT

"You shall have no other gods before me."
(Ex. 20:3; Dt. 5:7)

A. Exposition

Following Calvin, we will deal first with the negative version of the commandment in the Old Testament and New Testament and then with the positive version in the Old Testament and New Testament respectively.

1) The Negative Version in the Old Testament

Where in the Old Testament, besides Exodus 20 and Deuteronomy 5, do negative versions of this commandment occur? We begin with this question because it is through exposition of these passages that we will be able to delineate this commandment's full range of meaning. We shall, by practising a little trick of exposition, note the verbs especially; they will, more than any other linguistic element, be the key to interpreting what it means to have other gods.

Old Testament commandments usually find their first interpretation in the Book of the Covenant (the penal law code which follows immediately after the Decalogue. The name "Book of the Covenant" occurs in Exodus 24:7). Exodus 22:20 talks, in the context of fit punishment, about "whoever sacrifices to any god other than the LORD." Exodus 23:13 warns that we are not to "invoke the names of other gods." Like a litany of apostasy, Joshua 23:7 gives a series of verbs denoting worship of other gods: to invoke, to swear by, to serve, to bow down to. Deuteronomy recognizes that the temptation "to worship other gods, bowing down to them" (17:3) or to "follow other gods" (Dt. 11:28) may come from one's own heart as well as from the seductive example of pagan neighbours.

The first commandment is also discussed in the context of its breach. Hosea 13:4 repeats the commandment in the midst of stark descriptions of Israel's failure to uphold it. And we are given, in the context of Judah's impending destruction, a vivid picture of what it means to transgress the first commandment: Jeremiah 7:18 describes a whole family engaged in idolatry. These are, the Bible declares, people of God's possession and so they must face His jealousy and wrath.

So we have a legal codification, an exhortation, and an accusation of a trespass already occurring, and, as well, some occasions of dramatic repentance and the abolition of worship of other gods. An example of this last is Joshua at Shechem (Jos. 24:23), where he tells the people to "Throw away the foreign gods ... and yield your hearts to the LORD, the God of Israel."

The first commandment in the Old Testament covers not only crude, palpable transgression, but the spiritual one as well. Habakkuk describes the militarism of the Chaldeans. In Habakkuk 1:16, he describes idolatry as greed and avarice, the adoration of the spoils of war. Even more to the point is Samuel's reproach of Saul, "to obey is better than sacrifice" (1 Sam. 15:22). Disobedience is idolatry. It is the worship of self-will, that alien god which is closest to our heart. The first commandment is perhaps not so much concerned with monotheism as monolatry: it seeks to ensure that only the one God is being served. The interest here is not so much on metaphysics as it is on the practical question of service and obedience. The theoretical question of the existence of other gods is not the main issue.

Finally, we are to have "no other gods besides / in spite of / in defiance of / to the disadvantage of / to the neglect of me." Again, the dominant issue here is God's jealousy; the constant battle for the exclusive sovereignty of God. His incomparable majesty does not allow any division of man's allegiance. "For the Lord your God is a consuming fire, a jealous God" (Dt. 4:24; cf. Heb. 12:29).

2. The Negative Version in the New Testament

There are several examples of the negative version in the New Testament. In Acts 17:16 we are told that Paul was "greatly distressed as he saw the city of Athens abandoned to idolatry. Galatians 4:8 declares that "Formerly, when you did not know God, you were slaves to those who by nature are not gods." 1 Corinthians 12:2 speaks of "mute idols" and, in the same letter, we are reminded that "for us there is but one God, the Father" (1 Cor. 8:6). Polytheism or pantheism are not options: We must worship God alone. The Club of Rome's preparation for a pantheistic world religion cannot be reconciled with biblical monotheism. 1 Corinthians 10:14 tells us to "flee from idolatry" (cf. 1 Jn. 5:21). Idolatry appears in the lists of sins which exclude one from the kingdom (Gal. 5:20; 1 Cor. 6:9). "You cannot," Christ warned, "serve both God and mammon" (Lk. 16:13). And, in the same way as we saw in the Old Testament, idolatry in the New Testament also includes greed and avarice (Eph. 5:5). One who is covetous is an idolater.

3. The Positive Version in the Old Testament

The first commandment is not fulfilled by a statement of monotheism. We do not satisfy the demands of the commandment by merely professing a belief in the existence of one God. Such a statement could be a cool proposition, spoken from a position of neutrality. But the commandment leaves no room for neutrality: We are to cleave to the Lord, to love him. What is needed is not just a shunning of idols, but a passionate turning toward the one God. We are to be "very zealous for the LORD God Almighty" (1 Kings 19:10), to have a "zeal for your [God's] house" (Ps. 69:9).

To love God, wholly and alone, is to fulfil the first commandment. Here is a remarkable affinity between the Old Testament and the writings of John (cf. Jn 14:15; 15:10). In both, to love God is to keep his commandments. Deuteronomy, emphasizing the deepness of our dedication, says that this love is to be "with all your heart" (Dt. 6:5). Joshua 22:5 summarizes the details of our devotedness to God:

> "Be very careful to keep the commandment the LORD, your God, to walk in all his ways, to obey his commands, to hold fast to him and to serve him with all your heart and all your soul."

Biblical faith is manifested by the way one lives.

Keeping the commandment is equated with conversion (Dt. 30:10). The positive fulfilment of the first commandment is "to seek him [the LORD] with all their heart" (Ps. 119:2; Jer. 29:13-14). The concrete realization of the first commandment, prayer, is the proof of faith (Ps 119:58). The practical positive equivalent to "no other gods" is the prayer of the boy Samuel (1 Sam. 3:10): "Speak for your servant is listening."

4. The Positive Version in the New Testament

The New Testament has at its core this simple assertion: "yet for us there is but one God." (1 Cor. 8:6). Christ, rebuking Satan in the desert, declared, "Worship the Lord your God, and serve him only" (Mt. 4:10)—an echo of Deuteronomy 6:13, but without Deuteronomy's injunction to also fear God. The *Shema* (Dt. 6:5) is incorporated into Jesus' declaration of the greatest commandment (Mt. 22:37-39). "With all your heart," the Old Testament phrase, is also found in the New Testament: in relation to how we believe (Acts 8:37)[1], how we hope (1 Pet. 1:13), and how we love (Mt. 22:37), which is the triad of 1 Corinthians 13:13.

Paul uses the dative of advantage or disadvantage to express the reciprocity of commitment between men and God: "And he died for all that those who live should...live for him who died for them" (2 Cor. 5:15). The aim of Christ's saving work is a change of direction in a person's way of living, a change of loyalty.

In summary, the New Testament contains many instances of the positive version of the first commandment. It is especially prominent in the first three petitions of the Lord's Prayer. This, in fact, is the fullest interpretation of the positive equivalent of the commandment in the New Testament. To pray this prayer and to live this prayer is to fulfil, in all loyalty, passion and commitment to the Lord, the commandment to have no other gods before Him.

---

[1] This verse is placed in the margin in the NIV [ed.note]

B. A Meditation on the Functions of the Commandments

I have in mind here the effects of all the commandments, but I will use the first commandment by way of example. There are at least three functions: a critical one, a liberating one, and a commanding one.

1) The Critical Function

As soon as man hears the first commandment, he responds with apostasy and idolatry: While Moses is receiving the Decalogue, Israel is worshipping the golden calf (Ex. 32). That is a symptom of man's fallenness. Man cannot react to what he hears with neutrality. He no longer has a choice. Sin binds mankind to acts of betrayal and rebellion. Man's transgression is a settled fact about him; the commandment simply accuses, uncovers the sin.

The first commandment is always a call to repentance because we are rarely single-minded in our commitment to God. The commandment, taken seriously, produces the response: God be merciful to me, a sinner. Although Israel, through God's delivering them from their Egyptian bondage, experienced God's goodness in a brilliant way, they still threw their lot in with other gods, even though such gods do not exist. This is man's general tendency. Man fashions for himself gods and then submits to them. He worships fetishes, things he himself produces. There is a sharp irony in the human enterprise of idol-making: half the tree is burnt in the fire and the other half, carved, becomes a god (Isa. 44:16-17; cf. also Jer. 10:3 ff.; Ps. 115:4-8).

Not only primitive tribes have fetishes. Modern man simply dresses them differently. Chapter 1,4 of Karl Marx's *Das Kapital* is called "The Fetishism of Commodities." The argument is that we make idols out of material possessions in the sense that we become dependent on them. The New Testament calls this, simply but profoundly, apostasy and idolatry.

But there are many forms of idolatry. Are pedagogues in danger of making idols out of books? Do we at times worship personality, gifts, abilities? Might ambition and the pursuit of success in a career be idolatry, a case of serving other gods? Is there such a thing as idolatry of self or of self-will? (If I say I shall do as I please, am I not, because gods are laws unto themselves, making myself into a god?) Is the program of self-fulfilment and self realization also self-worship? Do we build our images and enhance our prestige so that others will worship us?

Sex, success and security are, it is said, the three big idols, one of which everybody adores. Sometimes we worship all of them in different sequence, in different periods of our lives. Jesus speaks of worldly cares and worldly desires as things that choke out the Gospel, the worship of the true God, from taking root in one's life (Mk. 4:19). Into our confusion and our pre-occupations comes the liberating call from God: Don't! I am your Lord, your master, your measure, your commissioner, your satisfaction, your motivation, your security. The first commandment asks us to turn from our idols and turn to the one true God.

2) The Liberating Function

It has been observed that the worship of idols brings both pain and pleasure. It begins with the lust of submission and leads to the pain of servitude. What at first looks like freedom turns out to be compulsion and captivity. Certain acts have lasting consequences which determine our future choices. Charles Reade (1814-1884) said:

"Sow an act, and you reap a habit. Sow a habit, and you reap a character. Sow a character, and you reap a destiny"

Servitude can also consist of a spiritual blackmail exercised by the sins of our past which, like giant demons, tower over us, demanding tributes and offerings to which they seem entitled. This is certainly true of the worship of possessions. It may also be true of the sexualization of our society. Desire for sex becomes a gruelling coercion into sex. Into these entanglements God's command comes as a sword to cut us free from those things which, once embraced, begin to strangle.

It is significant that the original Hebrew text of the first commandment may also be translated as, "You shall not have other gods" (the strongest form of imperative), or "You will not have other gods," or even "You need not have other gods any more." This is true freedom. No person and no thing has the right any longer to enslave you. You are free as soon as you accept God's gracious commandment.

"All the past we leave behind and take up the task Eternal, and the Power, and the Vision."

God's promise and commandment alone safeguard the freedom of man. God's commandments free us from the oppression of the past and of things, of men, of circumstances. God is the one authority.

This also means redemption from the tyranny of fate. Nothing has the right to intimidate and terrify us. "I am the LORD your God." This is an indication of what is stated explicitly in the New Testament: "Cast all your anxiety on him because he cares for you" (1 Pet. 5:7; cf. Phil. 4:6). Instead of worrying, pray!

God's promise and commandment free us also from the domination of other people. In human experience, two forces of domination are common: others claim authority over us or, more often, we elevate someone into a position of domination over us. This can happen in all human relationships, for example, between husband and wife, between lovers. By "adoring" another human, we make an idol out of him or her. We make our own masters. We may even make our consciences captive to another person. Parents often play god to their children, or, reversing that, bow to their children's tyranny. They become idols for their children or make idols out of their children. There is good reason to suspect that a mother who dominates and possesses her son conditions him toward homosexuality. In all these situations we need to be freed by the commandment of God to not dominate others or to be dominated by them. We must never place ourselves in a position over others which belongs only to God. And we must never allow others to assume such a position over us.

God promises to look after us in the moment of decision, when we are torn between fear and hope. Left to ourselves, we waver between exultation and despondency, blithe optimism and bleak despair. Will I be successful? Will I be of any use in life? "I am the LORD your God" spells an end to such despair and perplexity: "I am your counsellor. I shall look after you in your moments of decision. I will show the way." That means an end to solitary decisions. It also means the end of the tyranny of fear and ambition. We often live hungry for success, trembling lest we fail, driven on by our cravings, driven back by our cravenness. We are ever anxious. The commandment, obeyed, means no more tyrants and no more devils and no more illusions. God speaks, saying: You are no longer responsible for success, only for obedience.

This is important in our families, even in our work for the Lord, our professional and social life. Even in the spiritual realm—in our life of discipleship, in counselling, in missions—we are not responsible for success, but we remain responsible for obedience. That should produce a responsible Christian lightheartedness! What God creates out of our obedience is His own concern.

3) The Commanding Function

That the first commandment does, indeed, command something from us is the necessary corollary to the comprehensiveness of God's own offer, of God's commitment to our liberation. The God of the Old Testament, unlike the gods of the Ancient Near East or Greek antiquity, who were tolerant of one another, is exclusive. The Roman pantheon was, in design, ingenious: It was the first to be built in a circle so that all the gods were an equal distance from the altar, a temple ready to receive all the different gods from the newly acquired provinces.

That would never do for the God of the Bible. Just the presence of his name is so exclusively powerful that when the Ark of the Covenant was placed in a temple with the foreign god Dagon, Dagon was found in the morning face down on the ground (1 Sam. 5:1-4).

Our God is intolerant, but He can help. Heinrich Heine (one of the great German poets of the nineteenth century) lived a very liberal and atheistic life in Paris. He referred to the sculptured torso of the Venus de Milo, the deity of beauty and sex, which is in the Louvre, as his "image of grace." He eventually contracted the diseases connected with her name, that is, venereal diseases. In a miserable state he went and stood in front of the statue. And it was as if she said to him, "Don't you see, I have no arms and cannot help you?" And so, being a Jew, he returned to Yahweh.

God's intolerance of other gods, described by Old Testament scholars as jealous holiness or holy exclusiveness, was proclaimed unforgettably by one of the greatest rabbis of early Judaism, Rabbi Akiba. Akiba was martyred under Roman occupation for refusing to sacrifice to the deified Emperor. The sacrifice as a gesture was insignificant: merely throwing a few grains of incense into a fire dedicated to the emperor. But it would have been a negation of God's uniqueness, His singular authority, His exclusive claim. Rabbi Akiba cited the *Shema Israel* as his reason for refusal. The Romans wrapped him in a copy of the Torah, saturated it with pitch and wax, and set him on fire. He died with a shout, "Echad!" (which means "One").

Because God's commitment is so passionate, man's apostasy and defection is so unbearable. It is the same with adultery among humans: It is the spurning of one's partner's deepest commitment. Thus, monogamy is the true picture of the relationship of God to His people.

But even when people forsake God, God stands by His Covenant. And He succeeds with His Covenant, sometimes even by brute, brusque means: Preventing spiritual adultery, for example, by sending His people into the desert or exile or captivity. He cuts them off from the things with which they compromised and defiled themselves.

None of this is theory, but a reality to be experienced ever anew. The whole of Israel's history is a battle over the first commandment. It is a history of God's loving approach and rebellious man's struggle to reciprocate. Each person and each generation is part of this history. We are all recipients of God's friendship and goodness. We must answer the question about our relationship with Him. What are the authorities we serve? What are we living for? Are we willing to love Him as He has loved us, with all our heart, soul and might? What is the present stance of the commandment in our church and in our nation?

A real turning in theology, church, and general culture is required for a fulfilment of the first commandment in our time.

C. The Love of God as the Central Content of the Commandments

1. The Loss of the Love of God in the History of Theology

The love of God is the true fulfilment of the first commandment. And yet, the idea of the love of God meets with some resistance in the Christian church. Some of this resistance is due to the captivity of Christianity to certain philosophies. Aristotle, for example, who has had a profound influence on Christian theology, taught that it was unsuitable (*atopos*) for man to love God. For him, God was not a personal God, but the First Cause of the universe, and one does not love a prime cause. Immanuel Kant, whose philosophy forms the base of all modern Protestantism, reformulated this thought by arguing that, we can only love someone whom we can perceive with our senses, so it is inappropriate to love God.

There has also been within Protestant theology itself much awkwardness in regard to the idea of the love of God. The Reformation, in reaction against medieval Catholic mysticism, replaced love of God with belief: We *believe* in God, and *love* our neighbour. Luther argued that we are not to try to grasp God directly, but rather to love him in His representations on earth, in our parents, for instance, or even the political authorities. In rejecting the love of God, Luther became a strange ally with his otherwise archenemy Aristotle.

For Schleiermacher, who represents the beginning of modern theology, God was not sufficiently personal to justify the idea of the love of God. In the generation following Schleiermacher, Albrecht Ritschl, the grandfather of all modern liberal theologians, thought it quite improper to cultivate that impertinent, sentimental familiarity with the Saviour which he saw so prominently displayed in evangelicalism. He demanded, rather, that we see ourselves as servants whose position is characterized by respect for and submission to God's inscrutable providence.

Following these giants, most prominent theologians of the twentieth century—the early Barth, the Bultmannian school, Emil Brunner—have repudiated the idea of man's love for God. Brunner's formula was, if not new, epoch-making: "God wants to be loved in the person of our neighbour", not in himself. That resulted in the now-popular reduction of the Double Commandment to, simply, love of neighbour.

In contrast, it is relevant that Karl Barth corrected, as he did in several other respects, his stance on this matter in his later years. He is one of those great theologians who, when necessary, are willing to criticize their earlier productions. In *Church Dogmatics*, III, 4, he acknowledges that the New Testament, especially the Gospel of John, obviously does speak of man's love for God and Christ.

Usually, though, the protestants have to look over the fence into the Roman Catholic literature of spirituality to find out anything about man's love for God. Hopefully, Barth's self-correction will lead to a rediscovery in Protestantism of a love for God. But Barth remains a solitary figure in contemporary Protestantism. We had better turn back from human theological traditions to Scripture in order to learn the essentials. Philosophical and theological prejudices can hinder our perception of biblical distinctives. We need to return to Deuteronomy 6:5: "Love the LORD your God with all your heart and with all your soul and with all your strength."

The phrase "love of God" is a genitive construction, and so ambiguous: it can mean God's love for us or our love for God. It must indeed mean both. God first loves us, and then we love him (1 Jn. 4:19).

2. God's Love for Man

God loves His people and makes it known ever afresh (Isa. 43:4; Mal. 1:2). God's love for people ought to be of great consequence. Because God loves and cares for people, fear is banished. God in His love is always near to his own. "[God] love[s] the people; all the holy ones are in [his] hand" (Dt. 33:3). His love is the basis of his relationship with man, of his sustaining and redeeming work.

In the Old Testament, God's love is compared with three relational attitudes in human life: a) parental love; b) bridal or matrimonial love; and c) friendship between persons.

a) Parental Love

It is fundamental to the Bible's teaching that God is like a caring father to his people. "You are the children of the Lord your God" (Dt. 14:1). This is also the message to Pharaoh: Israel is God's son (Ex. 4:22). He carries them like a tired child (Dt. 1:31). There is also the metaphor of motherly love, of passionate affection and attachment. But the actions of God are beyond human analogies. "Can a mother forget the baby at her breast?" This sounds at first like a rhetorical question, to which the answer is: of course not. However, she may; but God never will (Isa. 49:15). God's parental love and care is expressed in the metaphor "on eagle's wings" (Ex. 19:4), where the image is of the eagle catching the offspring on its wings while the young bird learns to fly.

Israel was called, adopted, educated, loved, guided. "I have loved you with an everlasting love; I have drawn you with loving-kindness" (Jer. 31:3; cf. Hos. 11:1).

If you know you are loved, do you need to be reminded all the time? We do indeed forget God's love for us, and, as Scripture amply illustrates, we need often to be reminded of God's fatherly loving-kindness. In the Old Testament, the reminder comes many times in the context of a prophetic call for repentance on the part of the people. God's children have become, not just forgetful, but disobedient. Only after their apostasy has been healed will the original relationship of trust be restored. Then God's love and compassion for his children will come into its own again (Jer. 31:20). Only when they have been brought back from their idolatry can God again identify with them publicly: "In all their distress [their Saviour] too was distressed" (Isa. 63:9).

It is not surprising to see the Old Testament background of the Fatherhood of God set at the centre of the New Testament. Jesus calls the disciples "sons of your Father in heaven" (Mt. 5:45). His parables teach, again and again, that we should think of God as our father. Jesus paints this with strong colours in the so-called parable of the Prodigal Son (Lk. 15:11-32), which should more correctly be called the parable of the Father's Love (so Joachim Jeremias in *The Parables of Jesus* (1976) p. 128). There is also the prominence of the idea of God as father in the Lord's Prayer. And John, in his first letter, designates God as "Father" without using any qualifier: God is, simply and beautifully, our father.

b) Bridal or Matrimonial Love.

The Bible also uses the image of matrimonial love to depict God's love for us. Hosea, Jeremiah and Isaiah all use this metaphor, which is well suited to describe the passionate exclusiveness of God's relationship with us: by no means can one let the other go. There is, clustered about this metaphor of matrimonial love, a whole group of related analogies. The first is found in the concept of election, where Israel, by God's choosing, become his people. Love elects, love chooses. Paul, in the New Testament, can say "as far as election is concerned, they [Israel] are loved" (Rom. 11:28). Love and election go naturally together.

A second analogy in this grouping is that of betrothal (Hos. 2:19-20; Isa. 62:5). A third is marriage, and, by implication, divorce. Yet God declares, "I hate divorce" (Mal. 2:16). There is no bill of divorce (Isa. 50:1).

The fourth image is adultery (Jer. 3:1, 2), unfaithfulness to the marriage partner. Adultery is, thus, an image for idolatry and apostasy.

The fifth image is the expulsion of the wife because of her infidelity. Yet the expulsion is only temporary, and the unfaithful wife is allowed to return (Isa. 50:1; Hos. 2:7). God does not break his covenant vows. There is, as has already been said, no certificate of divorce.

The whole group of images reveals the strength of passion involved in the relationship between man and God. God's love is not a quiet, steady, unmoved, static condition but plays out as a dramatic story. But because of the bride's infidelity, the story is deeply disturbing as it moves through all the depths and heights of emotion. The Old Testament ends with the promise that God's love will indeed reach its aim.

This metaphor lacks a strong continuity between the Old Testament and the New Testament. The image of marriage is found in the New Testament only in Ephesians 5. But there the image is reversed. Christ's love for the church has become the archetype, the example. All human love is only a secondary analogy of this love. The same reversal of analogy is found in the notion of fatherhood: "The Father after whom all fatherhood is named" (Eph. 3:14, 15). Man's fatherhood is, not the original, but the replica.

c) Friendship between Persons

The third analogy the Bible uses to depict our relationship with God is friendship. This analogy does not, however, occur in the Old Testament prophets. The prophets, indeed, were shaken by the unfriendliness and even hostility of former friends and by the hostility among men and between men and God. But God's friendship takes primacy in the New Testament. God, through the Incarnation, becomes the friend of man. Christ is, the Pharisees complained, a friend of publicans and sinners (Lk. 7:34). This is a formidable statement: The very Gospel coming from the mouths of Christ's enemies.

We saw in the New Testament that the analogy becomes the reality. In the Old Testament, there is always the proviso "like": God is like a father. But in the New Testament, the proviso is dropped. God is our Father. Similarly, God no longer speaks as a friend, but, in Jesus, is our friend. The distance has been eliminated. This change from the metaphor to the thing itself holds true as well for the Old Testament metaphor of rebirth. In the Old Testament, it was "as if" we are reborn. In the New Testament, we are reborn (1 Pet. 1:23).

Jesus speaks of his disciples as friends (Lk. 12:4; Jn. 11:11; 11:36; 15:14). Onlookers at the tomb of Lazarus exclaimed, "Behold how he loved him." Jesus encourages his disciples to approach God boldly as the tolerant friend who, according to one of Christ's parables, responds kindly even to our badgering (Lk. 11:5-8). Jesus begins this parable, "Suppose one of you has a friend..." God is the friend of those who obey him (Jn. 15:14). Our relationship with God is to be one of friendship.

Can we ever fully grasp this? Does the analogy even have meaning today? Do we know what earthly friendship is, let alone divine? Modern man seems incapable of friendship: he has lost the art of it. Perhaps modern war has hardened hearts, or perhaps the heartlessness of the technological age has made hearts cold. A biography of someone's life in the nineteenth century was a chain of beautiful friendships. Biographies in the twentieth century are often chronicles of rivalry and betrayal, of lost and spurned and unrequited love.

Modern man, then, is ill-prepared to deduce God's friendship from human friendship. Perhaps we need here once again to think in the reverse: to learn what human friendship can be we must study the friendship that Christ gave to his disciples. Again, with the concept of fatherhood, to learn true fatherhood we must study God's fatherly action and character. As well, God's loyal, passionate and exclusive love could teach us much about love in marriage.

In general, God's message of love is greatly enhanced and enlarged in the New Testament. The New Testament certainly connects the three images of parenthood, matrimonial love and friendship. God has chosen to be called our Father (1 Jn. 3:1). Children out of paganism are now no less than the elect of God (Gal. 3:26; Col. 3:12). They are ingrafted as a wild olive branch (Rom. 11:11-24). They are transferred to the state of adoption by the new birth. And this is no longer to be understood metaphorically.

But the New Testament also goes beyond these images of God's love. His love is not dormant, but alive and active and moving in history. Again and again the New Testament points to God's act of sending his Son into the world (Jn. 3:16). These events—God's actions on behalf of man and in the midst of men—express his love. His love is not mere sentiment and attribute, but action (1 Jn. 4:11). So we want to be careful when, for reasons of economy of language, we reduce God's love to the formula "God is love," even though Scripture itself does this. Otherwise, without due carefulness, we might fall into the trap, as some have, of treating the terms of the proposition as interchangeable. Scripture never does this: God is love, yes, but love is not God. Lest we are tempted toward such a move, we need to think of the history of God's love (Eph. 2:11-13). God's love is active. God's love has both continuity and activity (1 Thess. 1:4). God's love is both timeless and timely. It is both His attitude and His action.

There are other examples from the New Testament which show the width and depth of God's love. His love is extended to us even when we are rebelling and resisting it (Rom. 5:8). God loves even his enemies. His love is so sure and powerful that not even death will separate us from it (Rom. 8:35). It is his love which brought about our redemption (Eph. 2:4; 1 Jn. 3:1). God's love is so rich and overflowing that he does not keep it to himself. He makes it to flow out into us (Rom. 5:5). Therefore, His love can become the motivation for Christian action. "For Christ's love compels us..." (2 Cor. 5:14). It becomes the motivating power of our actions (1 Jn. 3:11-24).

God's love is seen in Jesus. As the Father loved the Son, so he loves us, and commands us to love others (Jn. 15:9). Even the nature of the Christian church is defined by God's love. The church consists of those who can say, "And so we know and rely on the love God has for us" (1 Jn. 4:16a).

It is, however, the crowning feature of the New Testament that God's love neither sprawls into a general philanthropy nor narrows to a slender shaft of affection trained only on the church. Rather, his love reaches out to the individual: to you and me. Paul witnesses very personally of the "Son of God, who loved me" (Gal. 2:20). God's love for us, for us as individuals, is the presupposition of and the prerequisite for our love for God.

3. Man's Love for God

Both the Old and the New Testament speak of our love as an answer, a response, to God's love for us: "We love because he first loved us (1 Jn. 4:19) ["We love God because..." in some ancient manuscripts, ed. note]. That terse phrase expresses both the presupposition—God has loved us—and the consequence—we love God. It gives us, in a nutshell, the substance of this excursion on man's love for God.

It must be noted that biblical statements about man's love for God are not as numerous as those that speak of God's love for man. There is not much to be said about man's love for God. In fact, the contrary idea—the fickleness and fleetingness of man's love—dominates the Old Testament (Jer. 3:19-20; Hos. 6:4). But the intention remains: "Love the Lord your God with all your heart ..." (Dt. 6:5). And the promise remains for the future: "...I am Israel's father..." (Jer. 31:9). But in the present, man displays little or no love for God worth talking about (Hos. 2:5).

The *Shema Israel* is the basic passage which speaks of—or, rather, commands—man's love for God, and it is echoed in many places (for example Mt. 22:34 ff). God promises blessing to those who love him and keep his commandments (Ex. 20:6). This finds its echo in Deborah's song (Judg. 5:31). Paul expresses the same confidence: "And we know that in all things God works for the good of those who love him" (Rom. 8:28). Those who are called will surely love him.

In the Old Testament, we find in the Psalms deep expressions of man's love for God. Love is, in the biblical sense, something that can and must be willed. It is not just sentiment. Love is, indeed, a feeling, but it is also an act of the will. That is the message of the Psalms: "I love you ... in whom I take refuge" (Ps. 18:1, 2). Here we find also expressions of love for God's commandments (Ps. 19), for his work of salvation (Ps. 40:17; 70:5), and for the place where his glory dwells (Ps. 26:8).

God desires love and mercy, not sacrifice (Hos. 6:6). Hosea prepares us for the teaching of the New Testament, as well as providing us with two new synonyms for love: exercising mercy and knowing God. Here we see the New Testament view that love, rather than religious scrupulosity, is the right and proper response of man to God. Sacrifice can be offered with little or no spiritual engagement. Jesus confirms this when, in response to the observation of the teacher of the Law that love for God and for neighbour are "more important than all burnt offerings and sacrifices," he declares, "You are not far from the kingdom of God" (Mk. 12: 28-34). Again, Jesus says that loving God is more important than the meticulous tithing of herbs (Lk. 11:42). The danger in religion is that outward piety might be scrupulously maintained while, inwardly, the love of God grows cold.

At least one parable speaks of man's love for God: the parable of the two debtors (Lk. 7:36-50). The parable is directed at a Pharisee on the occasion when, dining at the Pharisee's house, Jesus allowed a woman of ill-repute to wash and kiss his feet. The conclusion is, who has been forgiven a great number of sins will necessarily love his benefactor very much. Here we are given an important insight concerning the source of our love for God. Love for God arises from gratitude for forgiveness. The deeper meaning of the parable is that Christ, by God's authority, has already forgiven the woman for her wrong life-style.

The woman who poured perfume on Christ's head at Bethany, thus prophetically anointing him for his death, also showed her love for God. Love for God is practical. It issues in deed and action. Love means to do something good for someone. Loving God is doing something beautiful for God. These parables and stories in which love issues into action serve as paradigms for man's love for God in the person of Jesus.

Love for Jesus is an explicit theme in John. There, Jesus presupposes that people should love God and, consequently, himself as the messenger of God. But people fail in their love for God, loving themselves instead. They do not seek honour and recognition for God and from God, but rather they seek these things for themselves and from others. They lack, therefore, the one basic thing: love for God. If they loved him, moreover, they would also receive and love the one whom God has sent (Jn. 8:42).

Only in his small group of disciples did Jesus find such love and respect. Because the disciples accepted and loved the Son, the Father loved them (Jn. 14:21). There is a cycle of love and counter-love established here. We have already seen that Deuteronomy and John fit together in a number of respects, particularly in their shared emphasis that loving God, or Jesus, means to obey him. Love for God is shorthand for doing his will and keeping his commandments.

Further, there can be no love of God without love for one's brother. Jesus points us to our neighbour. Whoever loves the Father must necessarily love the Father's children. Here we are given another important principle: Love of brother is an expression of our love for God (1 Jn. 5:2). But note: Brotherly love is not a replacement for divine love, only an expression of it.

The Love Of God in Paul

Paul affirms that love for God is an integral part of our relationship with God. Love of God is practised and realized in prayer, where we cry out "Abba, Father" (Rom. 8:15; Gal. 4:6). Love of God is the true realization of that new relationship with God which the Old Testament promised.

Secondly, love of God surpasses the knowledge of God. Knowledge may be a source of pride and, paradoxically, the cause of estrangement from God. It may inflate a personality (1 Cor. 8:1-3). For the knowledge of God to be healthy, to be perfect, it must be matched with love for God.

Thirdly, Paul says love is the key to the last things, the eschaton. God has prepared unspeakable glories for those who love him (1 Cor. 2:9, quoting Isa. 64:4). They long for God's appearing (2 Tim. 4:8). In contrast to Immanuel Kant, Peter congratulates those who, though they have not yet seen Christ, love him (1 Pet. 1:8).

Love of God and love of Jesus is, as a fulfilment of the double commandment, necessary for true humanity, understood in the sense of man redeemed and restored by Christ and for Christ. Love of God must be the aim of all Christian preaching, mission and counselling. People must be brought to the point where they begin to love God, and they must be strengthened in such love.

This means in part that people must be encouraged to love one another. Paul assigns the grace of God to all those who love Christ in sincerity (Eph. 6:24). He even says that love for God is the criterion for church membership (1 Cor. 16:22): "If any one does not love the Lord, a curse be on him," let him be excluded. Here is an answer to the frequently asked question about where the boundaries of the church are.

This also speaks, again, of the exclusiveness of divine and Christly love. Friendship with the world is, necessarily, enmity towards God (1 Jn. 2:15; Jas. 4:4). There are people like Demas who have come to love the world (2 Tim. 4:10).

Because love of God is such a field of tension, of final decisions, all love for God will be accompanied by fear of God, a fear borne of respect for God's holiness. Who then can love God? True love of God is impossible for man. We need God's intervention throughout: "May the Lord direct your hearts into God's love and Christ's perseverance" (2 Thess. 3:5).

Two Practical Applications

We will conclude this excursion by looking at two practical applications of the love of God: *prayer*, and *obedience*.

First, let us consider *prayer*. Love sustains communication. Love of God must be practiced as a continuous dialogue or conversation. In friendship one takes time exclusively with the other. In friendship and love, one shares one's plans, one's hopes, thoughts and disappointments. There are times of sustained intimacy and times, too, for the short, quick call from work.

Thomas Aquinas, following Aristotle, defined friendship with God as well-wishing, well-doing and spiritual union. That is a great definition of human friendship, but we may wonder whether well-wishing and well-doing have any place in our relationship with God. Spiritual union, the third characteristic, however, clearly applies to our love for God and describes what it must be. We see this quality in Jesus. His life is the prototype of love for God and therefore the prototype of the fulfilment of the first commandment. In thought and in will, he is completely united with the Father. Even in decisions difficult for the human mind to accept, Jesus identifies wholly with God's plan and practice (Mt. 11:20-26).

If we take Jesus' example seriously we must stress dialogue as a central characteristic of prayer. Among Protestants, our understanding is generally poor on this point. We take prayer as a monologue to God: "one-way prayer." We must, though, also listen to God. He may speak to us through the Bible and the Holy Spirit. Love of God, therefore, means a constant close contact with Scripture and a prayerful, meditating reading of it to become steeped in the mind of Christ. We are invited in prayer to listen to God. God can give us personal insights, certainties, convictions (which, of course, need to be tested carefully by what is laid down in writing in the Bible by the same Holy Spirit, and also by the judgement of experienced fellow Christians).

That is the way the psalmist goes about it: "I will listen to what God the LORD will say" (Ps. 85:8a). Or, "The Sovereign LORD has given me an instructed tongue, to know the word that sustains the weary. He wakens me morning by morning, wakens my ear to listen like one being taught" (Isa. 50:4).

We recognize the same attitude in Jesus. We see the intensity, continuity and inspiration of Jesus' prayers. He is a man constantly living within earshot of God, ready to listen and obey. His essential decisions come out of prayer. He speaks of his motivation: "I judge only as I hear, and my judgement is just, for I seek not to please myself but him who sent me" (Jn. 5:30). He arose before dawn to pray (Mk. 1.35), and spent all night in prayer before calling the disciples.

We need to examine our own practice. Is there, in our lives, a similar expression of love for God? How would you judge the quality, quantity and consistency of your quiet times? I knew a Swedish woman whose grandmother greeted her each morning by asking, "How are you with God today?" That is a question we need to ask ourselves more often. Perhaps the only answer for some of us is, "Lord, have mercy on me, a sinner" (Lk. 18:13). Such a sigh would actually be the beginning of prayer and of love for God.

The second practical application we will look at is *obedience*. Jesus said that he desired not his own will or self-enhancement but God's will, and that is the most comprehensive revolution of human lifestyle we can think of. Our nature is to always seek our own interests, our own pleasure. But Jesus shows that to love God is to do his will.

To be sanctified and to sanctify oneself—that is, both passive and active sanctification—are necessary for those who want to live in communion with the holy God. But beyond that, the "saints" in the New Testament are, in the first place, not perfect, but simply "those at his disposal"; those ready to accept God's assignments and commissions. They are ready to surrender personal plans and wishes for the sake of following God.

To love God means dedication. It means to look after God's work and God's commission. God's love is energetic and expects energetic love in return. God's commission will always send us to people, to his beloved creatures. Love of brother and love of neighbour are thus the fruits of love of God, and are reliably rooted only in that love.

Such a reversal of the aim in our lives—such as dedication to God instead of to ourselves, practicing love for God, obeying his commandments—is the very purpose of God's saving work for mankind. The intention of Christ's death and resurrection is "that those who live should no longer live for themselves but for him who died for them and was raised again" (2 Cor. 5:15).

We need here again critically to examine ourselves and see where we stand in terms of our love for God. If his goal for us was that we should no longer live for ourselves but live for him, has he met his goal in us? To what extent are we at his disposal? To what extent do we live within earshot of God, standing by for his instructions, making his interests in the world our own? Compare yourself with Philip in the story of the Ethiopian eunuch (Acts 8). He was ready to obey when the call came, and so to be where God wanted him when God wanted him. His going was beyond reason. No one would ordinarily travel in the heat of the midday (except, of course, an Ethiopian, who was used to even stronger heat; but who would have thought of that?). It was obedient love that made Philip go. Later in Acts, we read the story of Ananias of Damascus, who, again obeying God contrary to reason, led Paul to faith (Acts 9).

How far do we let God determine our life? Perhaps our obedience is weak because our love is weak. Perhaps we care too much for the things of this world. Perhaps we live in a state of forgetfulness toward God. The first commandment reminds us of our true destiny, the thing for which we were created and redeemed: to love God, to listen to him, and to be obedient to his word.

For those who are ashamed of their lack of willingness to serve, of being at God's disposal, there may remain the humble request of the returning son: "Father, I have sinned against heaven and against you. I am no longer worthy to be called your son; make me like one of your hired men" (Lk. 15:18-19). We know that God will not leave us standing there, but will shower us, just as Jesus described it in the parable of the prodigal son, with gifts to live a new life.

There are, then, two practical applications of love of God: *prayer* and *obedience*. They come together in an exemplary fashion in Mary, the mother of Jesus, who can therefore be a model for us. She possessed the combination of love for God and a readiness to obey. On the one hand she says, "I am the Lord's servant,... may it be to me as you have said," and on the other hand she joyfully exclaims, "My spirit rejoices in God my Saviour" (Lk. 1:38, 47).

THE SECOND COMMANDMENT

"You shall not make for yourself an idol in the form of anything in heaven above or on the earth beneath or in the waters below. You shall not bow down to them or worship them, for I, the Lord your God, am a jealous God, punishing the children for the sins of the fathers to the third and fourth generation of those who hate me, but showing love to a thousand generations of those who love me and keep my commandments."
(Ex. 20:4-6; Dt. 5:8-10)

A. Exposition

1. The Negative Version in the Old Testament

A penal clause, spelling out the penalty for transgression, is not, unlike with most of the other commandments, found for this commandment in the Book of the Covenant. Nevertheless, this commandment is central to Israel's history. It stands out in the covenant renewal (Ex. 34:17), which, in light of the incident with the golden calf, is not surprising. The commandment also concludes the "holiness code" (Lev. 17-26). Leviticus 26:1, giving us a more detailed description of idolatrous objects, speaks of stone pillars, dedicated to Baal, or wooden ashera poles. As the first commandment ruled out other gods, so the second rules out making the true God into an idol.

What is the reason for the second commandment? It is the invisibility and the incomparability of God. This reason figures in the altar legislation: "You have seen for yourselves that I have spoken to you from heaven: Do not make any gods to be alongside me; do not make for yourselves gods of silver or gold. Make an altar of earth for me..." (Ex. 20:22-24). This is directed against the tendency toward the materialization and the earthly localization of God. It is intended to protect God's freedom. The Israelites are told to use uncut stones for altars lest they be tempted to carve symbols or images of God in the stones. This strictness is unique in the Ancient Near East. Neither beasts, fish, moon nor stars is to be taken as an image of God . "You saw no form of any kind the day the LORD spoke to you" (Dt. 4:15-19; 23-25). God, because he is invisible, cannot be fixed into a visual form by man. There is no analogy between God and the things of earth. Isaiah asks rhetorically, "To whom, then, will you compare God?" (Isa. 40:18-25). Any comparison is impossible because of God's infinitude and supremacy. There can be no analogy with the things of earth because God sits above the circle of the earth. In comparison to him the rulers of the earth are as nothing.

A curse is added to this commandment: "I, the LORD your God, am a jealous God, punishing the children for the sin of their fathers to the third and fourth generation of those who hate me" (Dt. 5:9b; Ex. 20:5). This curse is paramount in the curses of mount Ebal: "Cursed is the man who carves an image or casts an idol..." (Dt. 27:15).

The Old Testament adds that transgression of this command demonstrates utter foolishness (Ps. 97:7; Isa. 42:17). Isaiah 44:6-23 points out the senselessness of using the same wood used for burning in a stove for making an idol. The foolishness consists in making images that cannot see or breathe. This theme is powerfully developed in Wisdom of Solomon 13: 10-19: "But unhappy are they ... who have called gods the works of men ...." (belongs to the Apocryphal books). Psalm 106:19-21, commenting on the foolishness of the Israelites exchanging "their Glory for an image of a bull" (see Ex. 32), says the same thing.

The curse associated with the commandment has a double meaning. First, the people will suffer captivity, deportation and be in exile (Dt. 4:25-26). Exile is a consequence of idolatry: "Only a few of you will survive" (Dt. 4:27). Second, they will be given up to the very thing they have chosen, namely, serving other gods (Ez. 7:20). They are punished by a painful slavery to the very sin they themselves have chosen. "Therefore I will send you into exile beyond Damascus" (Amos 5:27), that is, they will be taken in exile to the place where the idols originated.

What was the outcome of the commandment? Idolatry did develop in Israel, as predicted in Deuteronomy. Examples can be found in Judges 17:4, and in 2 Chronicles 28:2 and 33:3. Idolatry was practised in both the Northern and the Southern kingdoms.

But, in answer to it, a battle against idolatry developed as well. An example of this is found in 2 Chronicles 23:17. The priest Jehoiada has Athaliah, who is on a rampage of murder, killed, and he destroys the temple of Baal and restores the proper worship of the true God. A second example is that of Josiah (2 Chron. 34:3-4; 2 Kings 23:24). He found the Book of the Law, and acted according to it, destroying all false worship. His battle was perhaps, for once, successful: No idol has ever been found in excavations in the layers representing the time of Josiah.

2. The Negative Version in the New Testament

In the New Testament world, idolatry was a present reality. The Gospel, moving out into pagan lands, encountered religions based on image worship, such as the cult of Artemis in Ephesus (Acts 19:35). Paul confronts idolatry wherever he finds it (eg., Acts 17:24-29), calling it "an image made by man's design and skill."

The reason the New Testament gives for opposing idolatry is, again, that God is beyond the world. God is above the world and so cannot be compared with things in the world. In Romans 1:21 23, Paul, echoing Psalm 106:20, expounds the theological idea that idolatry originates in an attempt to bring God down to earth: "For although they knew God, they neither glorified him as God nor gave thanks to him, but their thinking became futile and their foolish hearts were darkened ... they exchanged the glory of the immortal God for images made to look like mortal man and birds and animals and reptiles." Again, we see here the paradox, the inappropriateness, the perverseness of idolatry: that, in Paul's words, man "worshipped and served created things rather than the Creator" (Rom. 1:25). Because of such folly, God delivered idolaters to immorality and self-destruction.

The New Testament prophesies an eschatological return of humanity to idolatry (Rev. 13:14 ff). The characteristic action of the forces of Anti-Christ is to call once again for the making and adoration of an idol—the beast from the sea, which, as a historical novelty, is an idol that speaks.

3. The Positive Version in the Old Testament

Instead of idols, God gives his name to the people to be adored and invoked. In Exodus 20:23, God declares "Do not make any gods to be alongside me; do not make for yourselves gods of silver or gods of gold" because He himself has spoken to them from heaven. They are to make, rather, a simple earthen altar where he will cause his name to be remembered (v.24). The image is replaced by God's name, which itself dwells with them. God grants his presence by allowing his name to reside with the people.

After Israel occupies the land, she is commanded to cut down idols and then choose the place for God to put his name. "But you are to seek the place the LORD your God will choose from among all your tribes to put his Name there for his dwelling" (Dt. 12:5). So a substitute is given which ensures God's invisible presence. This was fulfilled in Solomon's temple, which held only the ark, but no image. Solomon is aware that even highest heaven, let alone the house which he has built, cannot contain God (1 Kings 8:27). Jerusalem is designated as the place where God's name resides—which is, for instance, reflected in Daniel's habit of praying towards Jerusalem (Dan. 6:10).

The positive side of the second commandment in the Old Testament is a call to faith in the invisible but nevertheless active and effective God. Man tends to have certainty only in what is palpable and visible. Exodus 32 reports that the Israelites thought "seeing is believing." Israel wanted a palpable guarantee of God's presence. But an invisible God is beyond manipulation.

Here God is demanding of Israel something unique. Calvin, in the *Institutes* II, 8, 17, emphasizes the educational value of the command: The invisible God requires spiritual worship. God calls us back from petty, carnal observances. This demand for spiritual worship began in the Old Testament, and opened the way for a religion of faith and trust, faith in his word and in his saving action.

And that is how God becomes concrete, through his works and acts of saving: "You have seen with your own eyes all that the LORD your God has done to these two kings" (Dt. 3:21; cf. Isa. 5:12: "...but they have no regard for the deeds of the LORD"). God becomes concrete in the facts of salvation history. The heavens are also evidence of the work of God's hand in creation (Ps. 8:3). The people of God are to seek the reality of God, not in dead images, but rather in the acts of salvation history and in his work of creation.

4. The Positive Version in the New Testament

In the Old Testament God granted that his Name should reside in one place, Jerusalem. Christ goes beyond the localization of divine worship, even if the worship is spiritual. He goes beyond the domination of the Name which characterizes worship in the Old Testament. In John 4:21-24 he teaches that God is no longer to be worshipped on the Samaritan mountain or in Jerusalem. "God," Christ teaches, "is spirit, and his worshippers must worship in spirit and in truth" (Jn. 4:24). And Paul teaches that, "Now the Lord is the Spirit, and where the Spirit of the Lord is, there is freedom" (2 Cor. 3:17).

Another positive alternative is that, according to the New Testament, God has given Christ in his image. Christ is the definitive image of the invisible God (Col. 1:15). "When [a man] looks at me," Christ declares, "he sees the One who sent me" (Jn. 12:45). But, we must note, the New Testament is strangely silent about Jesus' physical appearance. The desire to know what he looked like is a Greek desire. In the New Testament, though, the emphasis is on what Jesus said and did, on what he began "to do and to teach" (Acts 1:1). So in order to know what God is like, we do not speculate or reason, but rather look to Jesus, obediently listening to what he tells us about himself.

The New Testament letters contain other material regarding the invisibility of God. "So we fix our eyes not on what is seen but on what is unseen. For what is seen is temporary, but what is unseen is eternal" (2 Cor. 4:18). Faith sees him who is invisible (Heb. 11:1). Such faith is our source of perseverance. Such faith also applies to Jesus Christ, whom the faithful love, even though at present they do not see him (1 Pet. 1:8).

God's invisibility, his transcendence, needs to be complemented in the New Testament just as it was in the Old Testament. The New Testament is not interested in mere metaphysical pronouncements. And so the teaching about God's invisibility concerns not so much his transcendence as it does his future acts. Faith in the invisible is faith in God's promises. Faith spans the distance between promise and fulfilment. This is seen clearly in Hebrews 11:1: "Now faith is being sure of what we hope for and certain of what we do not see." Biblical faith, then, is not primarily a faith in a transcendent being but rather trust in God's future action. It is a looking forward to God's fulfilment of his promises.

B. Meditation on the Prohibition of Imagery

We will, once again, look at the critical and the liberating effects of the commandment. This commandment is directed, not just against molten or graven images, but also against mental images we have of God. As Martin Buber said, "The fight against this [the attempt to reduce the Divinity to a form available for and identifiable by the senses] is a fight to subdue the revolt of fantasy against faith. ...it is necessary to recognize Him as He is, and not in the shape with which people would like to endow Him." (Martin Buber, *Moses* (1946) pp. 127, 132).

Idolatry is secretly a reversal of the God-Man relationship. It makes man the decisive factor. The idolater is the man who determines what God is going to be. Think, for example, of the Jews whose idea of the coming Messiah blinded them to Christ.

But that is symptomatic of us all: The entire history of mankind is an attempt to redefine the image of God. The workshops for this mental drawing and melting and engraving are the Arts and Theology. These areas are especially vulnerable to the temptation to mental idolatry. The tendency is to do a little mental touching up of the biblical image of God.

One classic example is the nineteenth century removal of the concept of the wrath of God. Schleiermacher said, "This does not in the least mean that previously he [humankind in general] was the object of divine displeasure or wrath, for there is no such object." (*The Christian Faith*, second volume (1963) p. 503). The concept of God is continually being refashioned according to the whims of man. Some today say, "Cut off the upper half of God. We don't accept a transcendental God any longer. Reduce him to the religious code for brotherly love. Do away with his transcendence."

Theology consists in making distinctions and passing judgments. But it is highly arrogant for us to decide how God must be. The problem is not confined to academics: It is rather a lack of piety in general. Cutting God down to our own size, within the range of our imaginative faculty, is idolatry too (see Calvin's *Institutes*, I, 11, 4).

Why is the attempt to limit God so awful? Because we then miss the splendour and beauty of the true God (Ps. 14:1-3;53:2-4; 36:7). The psalmist declares, "Your love is better than life..." (Ps. 63:3). Were we to attempt to shrink God down to human size, this greatest, this most vivid, experience of joy would be forfeited. A plaster figure is incapable of providing new experience, and it soon becomes boring. An image trimmed to the size of its maker soon reveals its limitations. A god made in a human image is by its nature dead.

An idol leads a man, by necessity, into loneliness. An idol leads man into loneliness, when what man needs is a God with whom he can have dialogue. A mere image of God is a mirror image of god: It is man's own image, reflected back. Such a god answers only in echoes.

The decisive point is, again, that idols infringe upon God's sovereignty and freedom. The commandment prohibiting idolatry is a commandment for God to remain himself. Thus, it liberates us from our religious limitations. Man's tendency is to keep God and himself small by making images of both. Calvin writes, "How great is our inborn tendency to idolatry. Like the water which breaks forth from a large well ...." (*Institutes* I, 2, 3). But God, by His grace, gives us this commandment to prevent us from inflicting spiritual blindness on ourselves. This commandment opens wide the door through which God leads us far beyond our earth-bound expectations.

An aside is necessary here. This commandment destroys the basic premise of modern time's most devastating critique of religion: Ludwig Feuerbach's "projection theory of religion." Feuerbach was a famous critic of religion whose method was adopted by Karl Marx. He said that man is not the image of God, but God is the image of man. The second commandment guards against such a thing, and shatters Feuerbach's critique.

There is a reversal of this commandment, and it has a liberating effect. God actually makes for himself an image of man, or, rather, two images. First, God sees man as he really is: "The Lord looks down from heaven ... there is no one who does good, not even one" (Ps. 14:1-3; cf. Rom. 3:1-12). But God sees man also at his best. Jesus says, in the context of a compliment to Nathaniel, "I saw you while you were still under the fig tree before Philip called you" (Jn. 1:48). He sees us as we really are.

But, secondly, he also sees us as we were meant to be. He sees our destiny. In Jesus Christ, God has provided an image of what man is truly to be under God. Christ is not only the true image of God, but also the "true man." He is the prototype of the new man. It is this image of true manhood under God as shown in Christ that is also our destiny: "For those God foreknew he also predestined to be conformed to the likeness of his Son ...." (Rom. 8:29; cf. 2 Cor. 3:18; Col. 3:10). We are all being changed into Christ's image by the Spirit of the Lord.

THE THIRD COMMANDMENT

"You shall not misuse the name of the Lord Your God, for the Lord will not hold anyone guiltless who misuses his name." (Ex. 20:7; Dt. 5:11)

This is the third commandment by Calvin's counting, the second by the Catholic or Lutheran counting.

A. Exposition

1. The Negative Version in the Old Testament

The commandment has three primary offenses in view: the false oath, blasphemy, and magic.

The first offence is false oaths. In Leviticus 19:12, in the context of the holiness code (itself an exposition of the Decalogue), we read, "Do not swear falsely by my name and so profane the name of your God." In the Old Testament, the invocation of God's name always plays a part in making a strong statement. Thus, a profane usage of God's name would be using his name to endorse a lie, or swearing deceitfully by it (cf. Ps. 24:4).

The second offence is blasphemy. It, too, is dealt with in the holiness code (Lev. 24:16), and had, as the sanctioned penalty, death by stoning.

The third offence is use of God's name in magic. Ancient Near Eastern texts abound with references to magic. The practice was widespread in those cultures surrounding the Israelites.

What is the reason for this commandment? The background for it is Exodus 3:14, the giving of the divine name, "I AM WHO I AM." To give a name is to grant access to that person. It is the same thing as establishing a relationship. It is like being given the Prime Minister's private phone number, which is an invitation to make use of it and call him. It is the same with God: The revelation of the name is the key to the holy of holies. That is why God takes measures to safeguard its proper use. So a good translation of the commandment would be, "You shall not use God's name in vain, inappropriately, improperly, trivially, idly, in an empty manner." God's majesty demands that kind of respect for his name. To use his name non-sensically would make him the same as the idols (1 Cor. 8:4).

The commandment must be understood against the Old Testament and Ancient Near Eastern understanding of names, where a name not only identifies but, more importantly, represents the person. It reveals his nature and calls up his presence. We see this illustrated in the Old Testament, where God's name becomes a substitute for God himself: "We give thanks to you, O God, we give thanks, for your Name is near" (Ps. 75:1). Psalm 76:1 has "God" and "his name" in identical parallelism. The name even becomes the agent of God's action: "May the name of the God of Jacob protect you" (Ps. 20:1b). Deuteronomy 12:5f makes an equation between God's name, his person, and his presence.

The same usage extends into the New Testament, where Christ says in John 17:6, 26: "I have revealed your name," (greek text) by which he means he has revealed God's fatherly nature. The New International Version correctly translates this, "I have revealed you." Christ, according to Philippians 2:9, is given, not only a new state in heaven, but a new name, and Acts 4:12 declares that "Salvation is found in no one else, for there is no other name under heaven given to men by which we must be saved." The Bible repeatedly makes the name and the person identical. There is no such thing as anonymous Christianity.

So, naming the name means presenting the person. Name and presence go together. Therefore, special precaution must be taken to prevent the misuse of God's name as an attempt by man to manipulate God. That is the importance of this commandment.

Avoiding the Name

In Judaism, the devout Jew, for fear of misusing God's name, avoided its proper use as well. This is an example of the ethic of avoidance typical in Judaism. There were a number of stages in the process. First, the consonants were left in the Hebrew but the vocalization was changed. The vocalization "Adonai" ("My Lord") was substituted for "Yahweh." ("Jehovah" is a mistaken rendering of the Hebrew consonants YHWH coupled together with the vocalization of "Adonai"). Today, some Jewish English writers are resorting to similar practice, where "G'd" is used in place of "God."

Further steps in this ethic of avoidance can be seen in the Septuaginta (LXX). The LXX translates Leviticus 24:10-16 to read as though the blaspheming man was stoned because he spoke the name of the Lord. We can also see this in the LXX rendering of Exodus 24:10, the beautiful story of the elders being invited up to the mountain to eat with God. The earth was like a sapphire on black velvet, an image which suggests a photograph of earth taken from space. The Hebrew text says, "They saw God" (verse 11). The LXX says, "They had seen the place where the Lord had stood." In the LXX, "the place" stands in for "God." In Judaism, even "Adonai" is being discarded for "the heavens" or "the Name" or "that special Name" or "the Holy One."

In the light of the third commandment itself, this practice is overscrupulous. The fear of misuse of God's name has given rise, by a negative ethic, to an avoidance of its proper use. This carefulness is honourable, but it makes for legalism and a loss of perspective.

But it also serves as a warning to those prone to carelessness in invoking God. The New Testament, for example, is economical in its usage of God's name. We find there both cautious circumlocutions and explicit invocations side by side (for example, in John 8:26 refers to him "who sent me," but v.40 to "God"). In Luke 6:35-38, Jesus speaks of God as the "Most High" (from Ps.9: 2) as well as "Father." In that passage he also, by employing the passive voice - "it will be given to you" (verse 38) - avoids using the name of God altogether. Elsewhere, "heaven" is used as a synonym for "God."

2. The Negative Version in the New Testament

The Jews' perception that Christ was violating the third commandment gave them the legal basis upon which they sought to destroy him (Jn. 5.18). He called God his Father, making himself equal with God. This was the pretext, or the occasion, which the Jews used to get at Jesus. We see this again in John 10:33, where the Jews picked up stones to stone Jesus for "blasphemy." The same legal manipulation is in the background of Christ's trial (Mt. 26:65).

3. The Positive Version in the Old Testament

There are many ways to fulfil the commandment positively. One which the Old Testament gives is swearing by God's name: "...take your oaths in his name" (Dt. 6:13). Invoking God's name in speaking the truth is proper use of his name (Ps. 63:11).

A second positive equivalent is to call upon the name of God. To call out to God in distress is also a positive use: "And everyone who calls on the name of the LORD will be saved" (Joel 2:32; cf. Ps. 50:15). Glorifying the name is another proper use. Scripture also tells us to use the name in praise: "I will be glad and rejoice in you: I will sing praises to your name..." (Ps. 9:2); "I will sing praises to your name" (Ps. 18:49; see also Ps. 103:1). Clearly, to develop fully the Old Testament teaching on the positive use of God's name would lead to an excursion on prayer.

Some of the other verbs in the Old Testament which are connected with a positive fulfilment of this commandment are to love (Ps. 5:11-12), to trust (Ps. 33:21), to ascribe glory to his name (Ps. 96:8), to fear his name, and to proclaim it (Ps. 22:22; Ps. 102:21-22). So proclamation is yet another positive fulfilment. And Malachi 4:2 really brings out what "fear" means in the Old Testament: "But for you who revere my name, the sun of righteousness will rise with healing in its wings." The fear of God holds out to us the promise, not of craven fearfulness, but of exceeding joy.

4. The Positive Version in the New Testament

The New Testament picks up all the Old Testament positive fulfilments, except for swearing by God's name. Praising the name of God is a positive fulfilment of not taking the name in vain (1 Pet. 4:11). The New Testament is more sparing than the Old Testament in its use of God's name. Instead, the name of Jesus is used (Acts 19:17). Or, as Ephesians 5:20 has it, we are always to give "thanks to God the Father for everything, in the name of our Lord Jesus Christ." This praise, this thanksgiving, is to come from the whole self (2 Thess. 1:12). So the commandment is fulfilled positively by giving thanks and praise to God through Jesus.

Secondly, the commandment is fulfilled positively by calling upon the name of God for salvation, "for, everyone who calls on the name of the Lord will be saved" (Rom. 10:13, quoting Joel 2:32, which is quoted again in Acts 2:21). It is, though, the context of the Pauline invocation that makes clear the nature of that invocation: it is calling upon the Lord in faith at baptism. Paul writes, "For it is with your heart that you believe and are justified, and it is with your mouth that you confess and are saved" (Rom. 10:10). This should be compared with Acts 22:16b: "Get up, be baptized and wash your sins away, calling on his name"; and with 1 Corinthians 6:11b: "But you were washed, you were sanctified, you were justified in the name of the Lord Jesus Christ and by the Spirit of our God." Christians are the same as those who have been baptized, which are the same as those who have called upon the name of Christ (Acts 9:14). They are those who have prayed to Christ, particularly at the moment of baptism. Calling upon the name of Christ is a distinguishing mark of the Christian. The church of God, the saints, are all those who call upon the name of our Lord, Jesus Christ (1 Cor. 1:2).

A third way the commandment is positively fulfilled is through confession of the name. Again, baptism is a form of this confession. Baptism is usually a public act, before witnesses, some of whom may hear and accept the Gospel through such public confession. Another form of confession is preaching. In Acts 9:15, for example, we read that Paul is "carrying" Christ's name, that is, preaching his name. Confession is the opposite, not just of silence, but also of denial; we are to confess Christ's name even under threat of persecution, when confession costs most. Persecution is the context of Matthew 10:33: "But whoever disowns me before men, I will disown him before my Father in heaven."

A fourth fulfilment of the commandment is prayer (see 2 Tim. 2:22; 1 Pet. 1:17). What is the name of the Lord in the New Testament? We do not find the name *Yahweh* there. Rather, the New Testament follows the LXX in replacing this name with *Kyrios*, "Lord". As well, the New Testament, especially where the context is prayer, often calls God "Father." Some systematicians say that "Father," rather than *Yahweh*, is perhaps now the proper name of God. We see in Jesus' own prayers an enormous emphasis on God's fatherhood, on his being "Father." Christ's prayers are, in fact, a rich source for true and proper use of the Name. He addresses God in peculiar fashion, calling God "Abba" (Mk. 14:36; cf. Rom. 8:15, Gal. 4:6). This is one of the few words in the New Testament that go untranslated [along with "maranatha" and the words of Christ on the cross: "Eloi, eloi, lama sabachthani" (Mt. 27:46)]. Joachim Jeremias has shown that "Abba," an Aramaic word, is a form of address which a four or five-year old would use. It is, at the very least, an expression of intimate affection, trust and respect. Such are the terms, the tone, with which Christ talks with God.

A fifth positive equivalent of this commandment is to hallow the name. Christ, in the Lord's prayer, taught his disciples how to pray and how properly to invoke the name of God (Mt. 6:9-13). The prayer itself weaves together the invocation of God with the hallowing of his name. To hallow God's name is to sanctify it, to keep it holy. This is the full positive equivalent of blasphemy or cursing.

In the Old Testament God himself will see to it that his name is no longer profaned. God himself will sanctify his name by re-establishing the people and cleansing them (Ez. 36:22 ff).

It is clear in the New Testament that Christians are to go beyond simply avoiding misuse of the name to an active sanctification of it. This means, in New Testament terms, not only to guard the name but to live a life that corresponds to the hallowing of the name. Christian servants who fail to respect their masters may cause the name of God to be profaned (1 Tim. 6:1).

Both aspects, the verbal invocation of the name and the hallowing of it through one's manner of life, are seen in 2 Timothy 2:19b: "Everyone who confesses the name of the Lord must turn away from wickedness." There has to be a practical dimension to prayer. Prayer is not verbal activity only: The God we speak to with our lips we must also hallow through our deeds. Our entire life must be spent in hallowing his name, which means we must be continually bringing God honour. This, surely, is Paul's meaning in Colossians 3:17, where he writes, "And whatever you do, whether in word or deed, do it all in the name of the Lord Jesus, giving thanks to God the Father through him". And the psalmist declares, "Not to us, O LORD, not to us but to your name be the glory, because of your love and faithfulness" (Ps. 115:1).

B. The Meaning of the Third Commandment

1. Reformation Interpretation

Calvin's and Luther's interpretation of this commandment are found in Calvin's *Institutes* II, 8, 22-27, and in Luther's *Large Catechism* . They interpret the commandment to mean not to lie, cheat, practice magic and the like, but, instead of these things, to pray, praise, give thanks and invoke a blessing on someone else. Those who acknowledge God in a deceptive way as a means of covering up evil, or preachers who pretend to bring a word of God, or false prophets, trespass this command. Our whole thinking, speaking, and behaviour should testify to the dignity of God's name.

2. What the Commandment Means Today

Today we see, in strong and colourful language, blatant and widespread violation of this commandment. This seems to be largely a male problem, illustrated, for example, when Peter swears and calls down curses on himself (Mt. 26:74). We also often witness today the casual use of God's name, where his name is used, like an exclamation mark on the page, for emphasis in speech. And, as well, we hear an unbelievable number of mutilations of God's and Christ's name: "Jeez," "gee," "golly," "gosh," "good heavens," "By George." All are an unwitting, and garbled, invocations of God's name.

A third way we misuse the name of God is in empty prayer, where we reel off pious words while our minds are elsewhere. And a fourth way is in jokes based on the Bible, which can be found in a Christian and in a non-Christian milieu. Both types are a misuse of biblical material.

3. An Appendix on Taking an Oath
a) The Oath in the Old Testament

In the Old Testament, oath-taking was simply a fact of the culture. To take an oath was to give God honour by solemnly speaking the truth. The third and the ninth commandment relate to oath-taking, which, in the Old Testament, was commanded (Dt. 6:13; Ps. 63:11). The invocation of God was part of the normal form of the oath in Israel, as we can see from Joshua's questioning of Achan in Joshua 7:19: "My son, give glory to the LORD, the God of Israel, and give him praise. Tell me what you have done; do not hide it from me."

This seems to have been the formula for giving evidence, illustrated, for example, in the New Testament when the Pharisees, attempting to wring a confession from the blind man whom Jesus healed, urge him to "give glory to God" (Jn. 9:24). In many places an oath is still accompanied by the invocation of God's name. God is the witness who has seen every thing and who is the guarantor of truth. Men, by invoking God, swear by one greater than themselves (Heb. 6:16). At the end of the Old Testament period, though, a hesitancy about taking oaths set in (Ecclesiasticus 23:9, belongs to the Apocrypha).

b) The Oath in the New Testament

Does Jesus reject the oath? In his time of temptation in the desert (Mt. 4:10) Christ quotes to the devil Deuteronomy 6:13: "Fear the LORD your God, serve him only". But the remainder of the Deuteronomy passage, which Jesus leaves unspoken, reads, "and take your oaths in his name." Is this, then, an application of what Christ will, in the very next chapter of Matthew, teach against the use of the oath (Mt. 5:33-37)? The evidence is ambivalent, for, in Christ's confrontation with the devil, the passage about oath-taking was not directly relevant to the situation. There is no need for Christ to quote it, and so he may have left it unspoken simply for this reason.

And yet, Matthew 5:33-37, as mentioned, contains an explicit command to "not swear at all" (verse 34). This teaching, as much else in the Sermon on the Mount, is echoed in James (Jas. 5:12).

This has been a bone of contention between the two wings of the Reformation (that is, the Magisterial and the Anabaptist). A full understanding of the commandment hinges on a clear definition of the biblical meaning of an oath. A passage such as Numbers 30:2 suggests that the oath was not a sworn testimony about some past event (which is what we usually mean by an oath), but rather a promise, a vow. It appears that this is what Jesus means by an oath—he is thinking of an oath of promise, not an oath of confirmation. Oaths of promise are difficult simply because no person has complete control over their future.

The Reformers, taking into account the context of Matthew 5:33-37, said that Jesus was not making an absolute prohibition of oaths. The context suggests that Jesus has in mind the private relationship between individuals, and that he is directing the commandment against the elaborate casuistry and the frivolity of oaths in that time, where the Jews (like children crossing their fingers behind their backs as they make promises) built into their promises all manner of loopholes and provisos to weaken the oath's binding power.

The Reformers pointed out that in the New Testament there are apostolic statements which come very close to being oaths, where God is invoked to affirm something. "In the sight of God, ..., I charge you ..." (1 Tim. 6:13; also, see 2 Cor. 1:23; Rom. 9:1; *Institutes*, II, 8, 27). These must be brought into account in any interpretation of Matthew 5:33-37. The Reformers came to the position that Jesus forbade the qualified, the voluntary, the spontaneous oath and the extra-judicious (that is, private) oath.

We have, however, the liberty to invoke God's authority over our "Yes" and "No", to call upon God to vindicate his glory and edify our brother or neighbour. Luther said that when our taking an oath is for the good and betterment and safeguarding of our neighbour, we should, if the magistrate demands such an oath, take it.

Today, the issue of oath-taking has been mellowed by Christian tradition and the protests of atheists. Nevertheless, many states allow, in regard to military service, a promise of loyalty in place of an oath invoking the name of God, or, in regard to court procedure, an affidavit in place of swearing to tell the truth.

While Matthew 5 is disputed, James 5:12 appears unequivocal in its prohibiting of oaths. A Christian should then, in all events, be slow to swear an oath, even in court. Wherever possible, he should use a simple declaration—"yes" or "no"—in lieu of an oath. There may, all the same, be cases in which the court demands, without exception, an oath. In such cases a Christian may take an oath in order to serve justice and his fellow man. For, while Matthew 5 is at the heart of the ethos of discipleship in the New Testament, that ethos cannot be made into a law of the land in a pluralistic society. While the ethos may be binding for the individual Christian, and binding for the church, it is not and cannot be made binding for the state.

This issue illumines the distinction between the general level and the Christian level of ethics. The issue of divorce makes clear the same distinction. Every marriage starts with a promise. But Christians cannot demand from the state a law enshrining the New Testament regulation against divorce. They cannot demand that the state outlaw divorce. But Christ's strong words about divorce and remarriage make the practice of divorce unacceptable among Christians. Thus, Christ imposes on the Christian a level of ethics distinct from, and higher than, the non-Christians' level of ethics.

THE FOURTH COMMANDMENT

"Remember the Sabbath day by keeping it holy. Six days you shall labor and do all your work, but the seventh day is a Sabbath to the Lord your God. On it you shall not do any work, neither you, nor your son or daughter, nor your manservant or maidservant, nor your animals, nor the alien within your gates. For in six days the Lord made the heavens and the earth, the sea, and all that is in them, but he rested on the seventh day. Therefore the Lord blessed the Sabbath day and made it holy."
(Ex. 20:8-11; also Dt. 5:12-15)

A. Exposition

The fourth commandment is, for several reasons, a point of contention today. It appears to be a piece of the ceremonial law which has strayed into the moral law. For the fourth commandment, by singling out a special time for service to God, has the flavour of cultic ritual. And is not the cultic or ceremonial law abrogated for Christians? Should not all times be set apart for God? And does the Sabbath law suggest that we are not to sing, not to praise, not to worship God on other days? Does it, in fact, suggest that our relationship with God is to be confined to a single day?

The commandment appears to have shallow rooting in the New Testament. Theologically, it raises the following issue: Is not the setting apart of a special time for worship just as inappropriate as the setting apart of a special place for worship? We know from Christ's discussion with the woman at the well, found in John 4 (esp. vv. 19-24), that God, being Spirit, is not geographically confined. Can he then be confined temporally?

The Sabbath commandment is at the forefront of the modern moral relativists' attack on the Decalogue. Christ, they note, never quotes this commandment, or at least we have no record of it in the New Testament. Further, they point to Christ's repeated debates with the Pharisees over this commandment, and point to Christ's words in Mark 2:27, "...The Sabbath was made for man, not man for the Sabbath," as Christ's deliberate trespassing of the commandment for the sake of love. In this they see a generalized warrant by Christ to break other commandments when necessary for the sake of love.

So the fourth commandment occupies an uneasy position in Christian ethics today.

1. The Positive Version in the Old Testament

The fourth commandment has a specific rationale: God, after creating in six days, rested on the seventh. "And God blessed the seventh day and made it holy" (Gen. 2:3).

The fourth commandment, like the second one, is long in comparison with the other commandments. It is, as well, one of the only two positively stated commandments in the Decalogue. This is further reinforced by the second positive commandment "six days you shall work" (Ex. 20:9) and by the negative commandment "on it you shall not do any work" (verse 10). In order to manage the enormous wealth of interpretive material for this commandment, even in the Old Testament alone, we will look at it one word at a time.

First, then, what is the meaning of the word "Sabbath"? It is, to begin with, not the name of one of the days of the week, like "Monday" or "Saturday" is. The word "Sabbath" comes from the Hebrew verb "to rest." So we could very well call the Sunday, the Sabbath, the day of resting. It means to stop doing what one has up to that point been doing. It means, to borrow Coke's European advertising slogan, "Take a break ...!" The meaning of the Sabbath is refreshment. As God rested on the seventh day, so too man must rest (Gen. 2:2-3; Ex. 31:17).

The word "Sabbath" is further interpreted by the Hebrew word "nephesh," which means "to breathe" and is the root word for "soul." The Sabbath is a time to breathe, to recover breath. 2 Samuel 16:14, the context of which is David's flight from Absalom across the Jordan, illustrates the meaning of Sabbath as a breathing space, a moment for refreshment. It means recreation, recovery of strength. 2 Chronicles 36:21 says that the land itself kept the Sabbath, its time of rest, during the Babylonian exile.

There are actually two reasons for the Sabbath. The Sabbath is not given just for refreshment, but also as a commemoration of certain events in the past. The deuteronomistic version of the Decalogue supplies this second reason (Dt. 5:12-15). There, the Sabbath is linked to an event in salvation history: the liberation of Israel from its Egyptian bondage. Servants and animals are thus the primary beneficiaries of the day of rest, just as the Israelites, when they were slaves in Egypt, benefited from God's act of liberation. "Remember," Deuteronomy says, addressing the free Israelite and the master farmer, "that you were slaves in Egypt and that the LORD your God brought you out of there with a mighty hand and an outstretched arm. Therefore the LORD your God has commanded you to observe the Sabbath day" (Dt. 5:15). The Sabbath is also then a reenactment of the deliverance from Egypt: Those who are under a burden are given rest, refreshment, and so can arise from the earth and, in a manner which befits a human, stand upright again (Gen. 3:17; Ps. 81:6).

The commandment is repeated in the Book of the Covenant, "so that your ox and your donkey may rest and the slave born in your household, and the alien as well, may be refreshed" (Ex. 23:12). The commandment here is directly connected with refreshment, and it is addressed to the free landholder. The beneficiaries are primarily the labourers, the servants and the economically disadvantaged.

The Sabbath, then, is both the symbol of and the reality for returning man to the freedom and the dignity of paradise, and the means by which man participates in God's own rest. And it is also a reminder of God's deliverance of Israel from Egypt.

There is, besides an opportunity for rest and a reminder of deliverance, a third meaning to the Sabbath. The Sabbath is a day which is made holy, is hallowed, is consecrated to God. To keep the Sabbath holy is to set it apart for God. The commandment to keep one day holy is placed side by side with the commandment to keep God's sanctuary holy (Lev. 19:30; 26:2). Even during times of pressure and business, "even during the plowing season and harvest" (Ex. 34:21), even during times of threat, the people are to set aside a day of rest.

This bright picture of the Sabbath has been highlighted by twentieth century studies of the Ancient Near Eastern religions. Representatives of the so called Bible-Babel dispute have questioned the exclusiveness of the Sabbath. Among many comparative religion scholars earlier in this century, there was, in an attempt to diminish the Old Testament's claims of uniqueness, a craze to trace back everything in the Old Testament to Babylonian documents. These scholars actually did find a Babylonian parallel to the Sabbath; yet the differences are more striking than the similarities, and the comparison only serves to make the Israelite Sabbath shine in an even brighter light.

In the Babylonian version, work on the fifteenth day of each month (or other days determined astrologically) was forbidden. According to the Babylonian astrological calendar, some days were days of commerce—with double the amount of work. But some were days of magic; they were dark, evil days, when work should be avoided. This contrasts starkly with the Israelite Sabbath, which is not a dark, foreboding day, but the brightest day of the week, when man is not warned away from working, but permitted to rest. In the Old Testament, the Sabbath is a gift from God.

The Israelite Sabbath, far from being a day of dark presentiments, is rather a day of refreshment and fellowship, a day of quickening. It is, in fact, a delight (Isa. 58:13). Judith broke her fasting, which was considered meritorious, in her widowhood for the joy of the Sabbath (Judith 8:6, belongs to the Apocrypha). A Jewish folksong says, "On the Sabbath, every Jew is a king and he feels like a new man." Jewish people began the Sabbath with a joyful fellowship meal. The following day, texts from the Pentateuch, the Prophets and a Psalm would be read. Those who wanted to study more deeply met again later and studied together.

The Talmud says, "More than Israel ever kept the Sabbath, it [Israel] was kept up by the Sabbath." The Sabbath was the means of spiritual sustainment for a nation in distress.

2. The Negative Version in the Old Testament

Exodus 20:10, we saw, contained the negative version of the commandment, "On it [the Sabbath] you shall not do any work." This was foreshadowed by the commandment not to collect manna on the seventh day (Ex. 16:19, 28-29). This passage demonstrates the second use of the law; it had the effect of showing sin, revealing the ensuing transgression.

The commandment recurs in the penal code. The penalty for breaking the commandment was death (Ex. 31:14, 15; 35:2, 3—where even lighting a fire on the Sabbath is forbidden). We have an example of this in Numbers 15:32-36: A man is found collecting firewood on the Sabbath, and is stoned to death for it.

The accusing use of the commandment also emerges in the Old Testament. The dominant passage is Jeremiah 17:21-23. The people, though commanded not to "bring a load out of your houses or do any work on the Sabbath," nevertheless disobeyed. The passage repeats the original commandment, but ties it into a context of specific violations: trade, the carrying of goods, turning the sabbath into a market day. Here we have the positive commandment—to keep the Sabbath holy—set side by side with the negative aspect of the commandment—not to work.

Ezekiel also accuses Israel of breaking the commandment, even in the time of wandering in the desert. In Ezekiel 20:13, the Lord names violation of the Sabbath as the prominent example of trespassing his commandments. Ezekiel 22:8, embedded in a list of accusations against Israel, states "You have despised my holy things and desecrated my Sabbaths."

There was among the Israelites a tendency to get the Sabbath over with in order to return to the business of illegal gain and the cult of acquisition (Amos 8:5). God warns that he will end worldly merriment on their Sabbaths (Hos. 2:11) The Lord considers sacrifices unacceptable until the people have cleansed their hearts and sin has stopped (Isa. 1:13).

On the other hand, some of the highest eschatological promises are related to keeping the Sabbath. If the Sabbath is honoured, "then you will find your joy in the LORD," and enjoy the fulfilment of eschatological promises (Isa. 58:13 ff; Jer. 17:24 ff).

In the Old Testament, the battle for the Covenant is the battle for the Sabbath. In fact, the Sabbath, along with circumcision, is a sign of the Covenant between God and Israel (Ex. 31:16; Ez. 20:12,20). The Sabbaths were continually being undermined by market days (Neh. 10:31; 13:15). In light of this, a belief of later Judaism is understandable: "If Israel would only keep the Sabbath once, the kingdom of God would come instantaneously."

The Sabbath is a gift, but it also a commandment, and both negative and positive versions need to be appreciated. The commandment serves as a critique of the way we live our lives. Are we not often so preoccupied with our own activities and plans that we find it difficult to appreciate the gift of rest? Time and again our work crowds out our time for refreshment. But taking a break challenges the heart that craves ambition. It challenges us in the midst of running the scrambling race for making money. It frees us from the relentless demands of careerism and the choking grip of fear. Those who are not hankering after sex usually pursue security with a similar passion. The Sabbath is a gift given to break such bondage.

But the Sabbath is not just a gift, but also a task. It is a commandment. We must work at it. And yet it is a commandment of grace. It loosens the demands which our circumstances place upon us, and restores to us our freedom, and halts us in our flight from our pursuers, and gives us refuge. It is God's gift of grace to us.

3. The Fourth Commandment in the New Testament.

The Jewish formalism of the Sabbath is the background for understanding the Fourth Commandment. Sabbath and circumcision were the signs of the Covenant and means of Jewish identification. Under conditions in which most nations quickly amalgamated and lost their unique identities in the host nations, the Sabbath kept the Jews intact, distinct. This was central to the life of Israel. We have also noticed the eschatological overtones of the Sabbath commandment. A common belief was that if only all Israel kept the commandment once, the Messiah would come, and he would bring to an end all of Israel's sufferings. In the Babylonian Talmud we find, in unbelievable complexity of detail, a great deal of Sabbath legislation (Sabbath casuistry is the second largest section). The legislation affected highly practical matters. In the Jewish wars, for example, Antiochus continued his military pursuit on the Sabbath, while the Jewish Maccabeans ceased from activity. Defensive warfare was, however, permitted.

Israel struggled throughout their history to obey this commandment perfectly. The excessive formalism which grew up around Jewish observation of the commandment led to legalism. Formalism and legalism, then, form the background against which Jesus' handling of the law must be seen.

Jesus was continually getting into trouble over the Sabbath commandment, or, rather, over the legalism and formalism which had developed around it. The Pharisees took offense at his picking grain on the Sabbath (Mk. 2:23-28), and at several acts of healing on the Sabbath (Mk. 3:1-6; Lk. 13:10-17). The problem with picking grain was not that it was stealing; Deuteronomy 23:25 permits the eating of standing corn from a neighbor's field but forbids the use of a sickle on it. So the crime, in the eyes of the Pharisees, was not theft but rather that Christ and his disciples were working on the Sabbath. Picking grain, then, was of the same category as healing: both were considered work.

Matthew 12:1 tells us that the disciples picked grain because they were hungry. This points to Christ's motive in all instances of his working on the Sabbath—the work was always done for the immediate relief of someone in need. Both feeding and healing were acts for the sustaining and restoring of creation. Christ, in doing this, recovered the Old Testament meaning of the commandment: liberation and refreshment.

This is illustrated in Christ's parables defending his actions. He speaks of a sheep or a son falling into a well, whose rescue would of course be permitted. The Jews, from ancient times to the present day, have clearly understood that in cases of imperative need or great danger, work on the Sabbath is commanded. Jesus, in rebuking the Pharisees for their hypocrisy concerning the Sabbath, drew attention to the necessity of feeding cattle on that day (Lk. 13:15). How much more does a man count than a beast?

Jesus equates doing good and saving life. He heals on the Sabbath for this reason: to sustain life. The sustaining of life is part of love for our neighbor. It is interesting that, according to the record of the Synoptic Gospels, Christ did not himself pick grain on the Sabbath, which emphasizes that his motive was, not self-interest, but concern for his disciples. The Sabbath commandment is primarily fulfilled through doing good. The act of mercy interprets the commandment. In a central statement, Christ makes clear that, not only are people to be healed on the Sabbath, but they are, like the animal loosed from the pole in order to drink, to be set free as well. And the Sabbath is the most appropriate day for such liberation (Lk. 13:15-16).

The synagogue ruler, when he condemned Jesus for healing on the Sabbath, thought that Jesus was acting merely as a regular doctor. This attitude shows the Pharisee's mechanical exposition of the Sabbath commandment. This is illustrated in their hostility to the healed man who carried, as a symbol of his healing, his mat on the Sabbath. The Jews were more concerned with not breaking the Sabbath than with truly hallowing it.

Here we meet again the ethic of avoidance, an ethic which, in contrast with the Old Testament Law, predominates the Mishnah. It contrasts, too, with Jesus' own ethic of fulfilment. The Pharisee's is a defensive morality, a way of barricading oneself against sin. Where such a moral code—one which is focused only on the bog-holes—has invaded Christian thinking, it has gone hand in hand with an absence of Christian goals in life. All that matters in such an ethic is keeping the boundaries. It provides no impulse for doing good. Rather, such an ethic, like a soccer linesman who only stirs to action when there is a breach of the rules or the ball goes offside, merely restrains evil, but never promotes good. We need, however, an ethic like that of the good Samaritan. The Sabbath commandment is only fulfilled by doing good on top of avoiding evil (Jas. 4:17).

Jesus countered legalism with love. Love for our fellow man is the gist of all of the commandments (Rom. 13:8-10). Christianity forges a third way between legalism and lawlessness. Paul makes the point in a surprising statement: "Neither circumcision nor uncircumcision means anything,..." (Gal. 6:15; 1 Cor. 7:19). The New Testament does not oppose Jewish legalism with Greek lawlessness. It preaches the surpassing, not the by-passing, of the commandments.

Mercy, redemption and liberation are what the Sabbath commandment is about. Jesus fulfilled the commandment. To obey the Sabbath commandment is to help, to free, to refresh, and to heal. An addition to Luke 6:5 reads, "Jesus saw one working on the Sabbath. He said to him, 'Blessed are you if you know what you are doing ....'."

B. Traditional Exposition in Christianity

Historically, there have been three emphases in the interpretation of the Sabbath commandment. There is, first, the mystical or supernatural interpretation. This is represented, for example, in Thomas Aquinas' *Spiritual Psalm*: Stop your work in order to learn trust in God. Obedience to the commandment is fulfilled through having a special Christian attitude, an attitude reflected in Psalm 46:10: "Be still and know that I am God." Stillness before the Lord teaches trust in the Lord. Calvin and Luther used this interpretation against works-righteousness, and went even further, into a mystical interpretation, by explaining the Sabbath with reference to Galatians 2:20 ("I have been crucified with Christ..."). In other words, to observe the Sabbath is to lay the old Adam to rest. The new man in Christ must arise from the Sabbath, ready to do God's will through God's strength.

There is, secondly, the interpretation which emphasizes the Sabbath as a day of rest. Luther takes the commandment as a piece of Natural Law, something which creation itself demands. Labourers, by design, need a day of rest.

The third interpretation emphasizes the Sabbath as a day for public worship and the study of Scripture. Here, a public consensus is required. From a Christian point of view, one day would be as good as another. Sunday has traditionally been preferred because it is the first day of creation, the day of the resurrection, and the day of the giving of the Holy Spirit. And yet the Reformers were not adverse to necessary work being done on this day. Luther has lists of jobs which are acceptable on the Sabbath. Neither he nor Calvin were sabbatarians. Calvin's later followers, not Calvin himself, were the ones who became rigid on this point.

A day of rest, a Sunday, is not a luxury, but a necessity. There are at least three reasons why we need this day:

(1) To confess our sins. It is a day for getting ship-shape: scraping off the rust and barnacles that encrust the hull, unravelling the seaweed that tangles the propellers. Only then will our original strength be restored.

(2) To enjoy, and perhaps restore, fellowship with God. A day of rest is a day for celebration, for loving God, for praising him. We are, of course, to seek the presence of the Lord at all times, but we must also set aside special time for prayer and praise. Prayer is actually a taproot of creativity. Only when the mind is relaxed can it open out into new ground. And Sunday provides us with the external circumstances for this leisure. It is a time for gathering new ideas, for probing deeper in our understanding.

(3) To enjoy, and perhaps restore, fellowship with our fellow man. Sunday is a time for common prayer and worship. We see elements of this in the New Testament. Jesus went into the Synagogue on the Sabbath (Lk. 4:16). When, as a child, his parents questioned why he had lingered behind at the temple in Jerusalem, he responded, "Didn't you know that I had to be in my Father's house?" (Lk. 2:49; cf. John 2:16). It is a day for exposition of the Scriptures (Lk. 6:6; Acts 17:2), a day for instruction and teaching. Sunday is also the day of Pentecost (Acts 2:1) and a day of charity (1 Cor. 16:2).

It is interesting that many of these elements can be glimpsed in the letter of Pliny, the governor of Pontus and Bithynia, to the emperor Trajan. The Christians, he wrote, rose early to worship, held a holy meal, and promised each other to lead holy lives. Sunday was a festive, purifying and liberating time. Secularism has levelled this day and much of the festiveness has gone. Services today often fail to provide refreshment.

In summary, then, Sunday as a day of rest is needed for at least these reasons: (1) to provide physical rest; (2) to provide spiritual rest (including the fostering of creativity); (3) to gather for common prayer, worship and instruction; (4) to encourage one another to be helped and healed.

Christian ethics has, and this is unique to it, a curative nature: it's salve for the wounded, balm for the sick. The Pharisees were content merely to be healthy themselves—or at least to believe themselves to be healthy. Christians are, in contrast to this, not to rest content wherever there is sickness. The goal of its ethics, and this is especially seen in the Sabbath commandment, is to heal. Albert Camus said that there are three kinds of people during a plague: the sick, the healthy and the doctors. Doctors are the important group, because they keep the healthy from becoming sick and help the sick to become healthy. Christians are to be doctors.

In light of all this, it is important to provide a mid-week service for people who have to work or serve on Sunday. And it is equally important for those who minister on Sundays to have one day free from all responsibilities.

The Horizon of the Christian Sabbath

Sunday is, not only the first day of the week, but also, as Karl Barth emphasized, the entrance door to all the other commandments which deal with people. This commandment presides over all those concerned with human relationships. That is the first horizon of the Christian Sabbath, or Sunday.

The second horizon is eschatological. Sunday hints at God's ultimate purpose for the world. It foreshadows the coming glory, and in a small way is an anticipation of it (Heb. 4:9; 1 Kings 8:56). One day all our diseases and woes will be taken from us. We will be able to straighten our bent weary backs and be kings and princes. We will be invited to the unending celebration which our best Sunday services are but a taste of. But they are a taste.

Now is the time to work, to bring home a harvest of fruit. We will certainly have to give an account for the use of the gifts He has given (2 Cor. 5:10). Through God's gift of the Sabbath, the day of rest, we must nurture his other gifts to us, to regather strength, to tap creativity, to draw inspiration. We must wait upon the Lord and after having received, give.

THE FIFTH COMMANDMENT

"Honour your father and your mother, so that you may live long in the land the Lord your God is giving you."
(Ex. 20:12; also Dt. 5:16)

A. Exposition

1. The Negative Version in the Old Testament

This is the second of the only two commandments in the Decalogue phrased positively. Deuteronomy 27:16 contains the negative version: "Cursed is the man who dishonors his father or his mother." The commandment appears to be addressed primarily, not to the kindergarten class, but to adults. As well, in the Book of the Covenant there are two clauses in casuistic style -that is, specific cases in which the law applies - where an adult is indicated (Ex. 21:15, 17). The death penalty for cursing one's parents is repeated in Leviticus 20:9 and Proverbs 20:20. For the man who commits such an act, "his lamp will be snuffed out in pitch darkness" (Prov. 20:20).

General disobedience is treated in Deuteronomy 21:18-21. That passage describes a "stubborn and rebellious son who does not obey," and prescribes the punishment of stoning, in order to "purge evil" from their midst. This, again, suggests that the son in view is a grown-up, a suggestion borne out in Proverbs 19:26, which describes the disgraceful son as "he who robs his father and drives out his mother" (cf. Ex. 21:15). These passages help us to understand the sort of child whom this commandment is meant for: the landowning farmer whose parents have become an economic liability. Between the ages of five and twenty years old, a man was valued at twenty shekels (Lev. 27:2-3, in the context of redeeming persons dedicated to the Lord). Between twenty and sixty years old, he had to pay fifty. After sixty he was required to pay only fifteen shekels. It was, then, the man in the prime of his life who had the heaviest financial burden, and so it was he who would be most tempted to abuse or turn out his parents. For such as these is this commandment given.

2. The Positive Version in the Old Testament

What does "honour" mean in the sentence "Honour your mother and father"? The Hebrew root is KBD, *kabod*, which means "to make heavy." So to honour is to take parents seriously, to place them high in one's order of priorities. In practical terms, this means that we are to care for them materially. We must be willing to give our money. But it also means to enjoy fellowship with them. We must be willing to give our time and our company. After the death of one parent, the other may suffer a growing sense of loneliness, and will have greater need of the children's companionship.

Leviticus 19:3 gives us further insight. Here, the commandment is related, through the full context of Leviticus 19, to the practice of holiness. Scripture demands that we fear our parents, that we stand in awe of them. The same term for honour in Hebrew is used to describe the proper attitude of the Israelites toward an inspired man of God (Jos. 4:14). The people understood the utter spiritual authority of their leader. The word also referred to the respect which people were to show for the temple, and, indeed, for Yahweh himself (Ex. 14:31; Prov. 3:7). Our attitude to God, the Bible commands, is one of fear and love.

The holiness code has other material which helps in interpreting this commandment. Baumgartner translates Leviticus 19:32 as follows: "Treat your parents with distinction." As well, Proverbs 1:8 reminds us that God uses our parents as our teachers. The Proverbs, actually, form the base of the Reformer's interpretation of the fifth commandment. Proverbs 15:5 teaches that obedience to parents will be rewarded in time. According to Proverbs 23:22, parents are to be respected even when they no longer possess powers of mind or body with which to impress us.

The book of Ecclesiasticus devotes the whole of chapter 3 to the theme of honouring parents: "God has made the father honorable to the children... He who honours his father... Despise him not when you are in your strength."

There is an eschatological aspect to this commandment. Our Old Testament ends with a pericope which is closely related to this commandment: "He will turn the hearts of the fathers to their children..." (Mal. 4:4-6). Family reconciliation will be the root of prosperity for the entire nation. Reconciliation is brought about by a changed heart, and this begins with the fathers.

3. The Parent-Child Relationship in the New Testament.

The negative version of the fifth commandment recurs in the New Testament in enumerations of sins—or example, 1 Tim. 1:9, which speaks of those who kill their parents. Among the sins which the New Testament says will be rampant in the last days is disobedience to parents (Rom. 1:30; 2 Tim. 3:2). Jesus quotes the commandment directly from the Old Testament in his reply to the rich young ruler (Mt. 19:19) and in one of his debates with the Pharisees (Mt. 15:4; Mk. 7:10; cf. Eph. 6:2). This passage is important in that it shows the disjunction between human traditions and God's commands. Christ says, "For God said,..., Anyone who curses his father or mother must be put to death" (Mt. 15:4). And yet, he points out, the Jewish tradition claimed that God's right supplanted the rights of parents: that children, in fact, should neglect their parents for the sake of rendering service to God. Christ dismisses this as hypocrisy. The text in which Christ's words are embedded shows that he interpreted the fifth commandment in terms of the child providing the parent with material needs. Jesus protects the generational links. In this light, it is interesting to note that Christ's raising of the son of Nain—the poor widow's son—also had economic considerations (Lk. 7:12-16).

It is the responsibility of children to look after parents and grandparents (1 Tim. 5:4). The smallest social unit that can handle the job should do it. "If anyone does not provide for his family, he has denied the faith and is worse than an unbeliever" (1 Tim. 5:8). Caring for one's family is a necessary Christian responsibility.

The third positive citation of the commandment is found in Ephesians 6:1-4. Here the commandment is, for the first time, addressed to both parents and children. The relationship between parents and children is reciprocal, each with respective duties. Paul unfolds the commandment in terms of mutual responsibility probably because of the structure of the passage in Ephesians:

He is laying out household instructions. Besides, he broadens the geographical range of the commandment's promise by changing "in the land," into "on the earth."

A shorter version of the commandment is found in Colossians 3:20: "Children, obey your parents in every thing for this pleases the Lord." Children are to honour their parents through obedience. Paul then goes on to address fathers, both in Colossians and Ephesians. In Ephesians, he tells fathers regarding their children to "bring them up in the training (education) and instruction (warning, rebuke) of the Lord" (Eph. 6:4). The first term, training, has to do with the discipline which engenders the good; the second term, instruction, has to do with the correction which averts the bad. This second was lacking in Eli, for example, who knew his sons sinned but did not restrain them (1 Sam. 3:13).

Ephesians 6, then, as well as Colossians 3, responds to the mixed bag of human nature. Parents have the difficult task of finding the narrow path between rebuke and indulgence, between crushing the child and allowing him to rebel. Only the Lord may be fully capable of such a task. That is perhaps what is meant. The genitive construction, "of the Lord," makes this ambiguous. It could imply that Christ himself is the teacher. Or the grammatical form here could be the objective genitive, which would mean that Christ is the object of the education. Probably both alternatives should be considered.

Other New Testament passages as well have positive things to say about the parent-child relationship. Christ, when he asks rhetorically, "Which of you fathers, if your son asks for a fish, will give him a snake instead?" (Lk. 11:11), implies that a father is inherently a provider and protector. And Paul states flatly the duty of parents to children when he declares, "children should not have to save up for their parents, but parents for their children" (2 Cor. 12:14). The view of the parent-child relationship which the New Testament presents is, overall, positive. It should be noted here, though, that these passages have younger children in mind. They should, then, be compared with passages such as 1 Timothy 5:4, 8, which outlines the duty of older children to their aging parents.

A good father encourages his children (1 Thess. 2:11). He also disciplines them: "We all had human fathers who disciplined us and we respected them for it" (Heb. 12:7).

Some of Christ's parables—the parable of the merciful father in Luke 15:11-31, for example—illustrate the special tenderness and depth of love that is possible in the relationship of fathers to children. However we must be careful in using the parables as illustrations of human characteristics. Sometimes, and perhaps Luke 15 is an example of this, the parables tell us not what is common among men, but what is unique about God.

Perhaps the real goal of the parent-child relationship is co-operation in ministry. This is seen, for example, in the relationship between Paul and Timothy, his "son."

4. The Eschatological Relativization of the Natural Family

Creation is surpassed by the Covenant. The commandment of the Covenant takes precedence over the creational order. Our loyalty to God must precede our loyalty to any man, including our father or mother. In this sense, there exists a tension in the Decalogue itself, between the first and the fifth commandments. We see this tension embodied, for example, in the incident where Jesus, as a boy, stays behind at the temple in Jerusalem, to the consternation of his parents (Lk. 2:49). But afterwards, we are told, he went down to Nazareth and "submitted to them" (Lk. 2:51).

The conflict continues in Christ's adult life. At the beginning of his ministry he speaks the brusque words to his mother, "Woman, what have I to do with you?" (Jn. 2:3). Jesus here refuses to be guided by his mother any longer. He is, rather, following the will of the Father (Jn. 5:30). And, indeed, his mother appears to recognize this, for her response to Jesus' rebuff is to tell the servants to "do whatever he tells you" (Jn. 2:5). This is an acknowledgement of her son's authority, and so it should not surprise us that her words echo Genesis 41:55, where Pharaoh, acknowledging Joseph's authority, tells the famished people to "do whatever he tells you."

Jesus, by ignoring his mother and brothers when they wanted to speak with him (Mt. 12:46), set creational loyalties—the bonds of blood and birth—in second place, behind loyalty to God. He recognized that a conflict of loyalties may arise in which the difference between loyalties is not one of degree—where one loyalty comes before the other—but one of opposition—where one loyalty must be chosen over and against the other. Micah sees this as an eschatological situation (Mic. 7:6). In Micah the situation is deplored, but Jesus sees these divisions within families as the purpose of his coming: "I have come to turn a man against his father ..." (Mt. 10:34, 35); "Brother will betray brother ... because of me" (Mt. 10:21). And this antagonism is not confined to the eschaton alone, but is also part of discipleship (Mt. 10:37). The demands of Christ override the creational ordinance. Parents must stand back and not demand to be loved more than Jesus.

Peter declares, "We must obey God rather than man" (Acts 5:29). Degrees of obedience are not being discussed here, nor are degrees of love in Luke 14:26: "if anyone does not hate his father and mother ... and even his own life, he cannot be my disciple." The Aramaic, as Joachim Jeremias points out, had no comparative, so comparisons had to be expressed in absolute terms. Matthew, then, renders what is meant here: "He who does not love me more than his father and mother is not worthy of me" (Mt. 10:37). Jesus knows that leaving family behind is like dying. It is carrying one's cross. It means giving up the pursuit of happiness for the sake of following Jesus. It is part of the cost of discipleship. Our first and our exclusive loyalty is to God. We all have different demands placed upon us, but the commands of Christ precede and, where necessary, supersede all others. The unconditional loyalty which the Levites showed toward God is, in fact, demanded of all believers (Ex. 32:26-29; Dt. 33:9).

This tension, this division of loyalties, is still felt today at two points of life: conversion and commission. Parents sometimes mount tremendous pressure to forestall their child from becoming a Christian. A similar problem often arises when a son or daughter hears a call to sacrificial service. The child, though, has the consolation of this promise: he or she will receive a new family.

5. The Constitution of the New Family of Believers

Jesus promised recompense to those who sacrifice for his sake: "No one who has left home or wife, or parents, or brothers for the sake of the kingdom of God ... will not receive many times over both in this life and the life to come" (Lk. 18:29). He established a new family: "Those who do my will are my brothers and sisters ..." (Mt. 12:50). Two of the seven words spoken from the cross are dedicated to founding the new household of God. "Woman," Christ said to his mother "behold your son" and turning to the apostle John, "Behold your mother" (Jn. 19:26, 27). As well, the apostle Paul spoke of himself as a father of one of the churches he had founded (1 Cor. 4:15). Yet, in tension with this, Christ gave a warning to prevent human fatherhood from arising within the church: "Do not call anyone on earth 'Father,' for you have one Father, and he is in heaven" (Mt. 23:9).

6. The Transfiguration of the Natural Family

Sometimes the creational family is transformed into a spiritual family. We see this, for example, in Timothy's mother and grandmother (1 Tim. 1:5). John Mark may also have received the gospel message from his parents, or at least his mother (Acts 12:12). The New Testament bolsters confidence that where the faith is accepted, whole families will believe (Acts 16:34). Families certainly played an important role in the early church. But, ultimately, it is not in the parents' power to make spiritual children. Sometimes they have to adopt spiritual children.

B. Present-day Problems in the Field of Parent-Child Relationships

Ours is the century which coined the phrase "generation gap", describing the conflict, open or latent, that divides each generation from the other.

Gustav Bally, a social psychologist, has said that the authority of parents derives from the authority of God. But in the drift toward atheism and agnosticism, parental authority has become increasingly arbitrary. Authoritative education becomes authoritarian education. Those sons and daughters who are not crushed by this arbitrary and unreasonable authority usually rebel against it. Earlier we saw a tension between the first and the fifth commandment, but here we see their essential connection: The parents who reject the first commandment can expect their children to reject the fifth one. The parents who do not submit to God should not expect their children to submit to them.

Sometimes, though, parents choose another way: they submit to their children. Dr. Spock recommended that, in order to change society, we must raise a generation which is uninhibited. This meant the abandonment of acculturation. Spock urged parents to feed the child, not according to fixed schedules, but when he wanted to be fed. The philosophy failed; Spock-children can be terrors. They are often tyrants accustomed to having those around them bend to their whims. Spock himself had the humility to admit, on British television that he was mistaken, and that children need authority.

Parents must dare to discipline. But they must also, when wrong, have the humility to apologize to their child. In this way, they demonstrate to their children that they, too, are subject to the discipline of a higher authority: God.

C. Other Relationships of Authority and Subordination

The fifth commandment has always been expanded to cover all other relationships of authority. The argument was that, on the earthly plane, there are three fathers: the human father, the master in business, and the ruler. The argument is unconvincing, but we will review it all the same.

1. Authority and Subordination in Work and Business

(a) The most comprehensive statement about authority and subordination in the work place is in 1 Peter 2:23 ff. Here, as in Ephesians 6, there are reciprocal instructions to both masters and slaves. Greek morality taught the principle, be good to your master and he will be good to you. But Peter goes beyond that, commanding slaves to serve well even bad masters (cf. Eph. 6:5-8; Col. 3: 22-25). The Christian slave's motive should be to do his work, not for the master's approval, but for the sake of the Lord.

(b) The Bible is not concerned with a slave's submissiveness alone: It gives, too, corresponding duties of the master toward his subordinates. The Old Testament is soaked with concern for the poor and the needy (see, for example, Lev. 25:43, 53; Jer. 22:13). Complementary New Testament passages are Ephesians 6:9 and Colossians 4:1: "Masters, provide your servants with what is right and fair...." That is the source verse of the Christian doctrine of the just wage. In Greek philosophy and legislation, which were the norm in the whole Roman empire, slaves were real estate, without civil rights. But many slaves in Rome were associated with a home and had major responsibilities, such as oversight of the household and the education of the children. Some of these preferred slavery to the hazards of economic liberation.

In Philemon 1:16 Paul asks that Onesimus, the runaway slave, be received back, both into the household and into the Christian fold. Indeed, Paul, with wry suggestiveness, asks Philemon to liberate Onesimus. They, the slave and the master, are one in Christ (cf. Gal. 3:27). Here we have a unique contribution of Christian ethics to social reform: Paul, like the prophets, is not instigating the lower classes to liberate themselves; rather, he is telling the upper class, the ruling class, to liberate them.

2. Authority and Liberation in the Church

(a) The question of Spirit and office plays a central role in understanding the relationship between authority and freedom within the church. Jesus warned the disciples not to call anyone "Father." We see in the New Testament, as a reflection of this, that Peter was not ruling the church as a second century monarchial bishop, but as being first among equals. Paul, too, recognizes this, speaking of Peter, James, and John as pillars (1 Cor. 16:15). But here we see that, though these men are not imperious rulers, there are clearly relationships of subordination within the church. Paul, for example, encourages his churches to submit to their elders. Paul's two criteria for leadership are long-standing in the faith and a simple commitment to the task. The New Testament makes a clear distinction between leaders and followers (1 Thess. 5:12; 1 Tim 5:17). "Obey your leaders," Hebrews 13:17 enjoins Christians, "and submit to them."

(b) The responsibilities of a church leader are especially emphasized in the New Testament. The burden of this responsibility lies in the fact that one day the leader must give account. But the Old Testament, too, contains some important texts in this regard. Ezekiel 3:17-21, for example, speaks of the guardian task: The prophet himself will be held responsible for the fate of those he fails to warn. And Ezekiel 34 speaks of the guiltiness of negligent shepherds, a metaphor for religious leaders. In the New Testament, we see James' stern warning that not many should be teachers, because of the heaviness of the responsibility (Jas. 3:1). Christ, in Matthew 5:20, utters the startling words that "Unless your righteousness exceeds that of the Pharisees and the teachers of the law, you will certainly not enter the kingdom of heaven." Among other things, the statement reveals Christ's concern about the frequent contrast between theory and practice in teachers, the gap between what one teaches and how one lives. The shabbiness of many teachers' example when measured against their lofty moral pronouncements brings disrepute upon the Gospel.

Those in authority have a responsibility to the church. Paul, for one, both emphasizes this in his teaching and illustrates it in his conduct. In his farewell speech to the Ephesian elders at Miletus (Acts 20), he may be alluding to Ezekiel 3 when he says, "You know that I have not hesitated to preach anything...." And in Titus 2:7, he stresses that leadership works best by example. Peter, in a passage from his first epistle which is central to this issue of authority and responsibility, sets forth the requirements for overseers (1 Pet. 5:1-4). Leaders must show a willingness to serve and to lead; they can not be greedy, and not given to lording it over those entrusted to their care but, instead, must give them an example to live by.

This passage from 1 Peter provides everything required for biblical leadership. Let us look further at leadership's three key elements.

1) The leader is not to squeeze the flock for material benefit (see also Ez. 34; 1 Tim. 6:9; 1 Cor. 2:17). There is always a danger of turning a religion into a business, especially in a society that can commercialize anything. The leader must never yield to this temptation. Thoughts of profit can not enter into his motives for leadership.

2) Leadership works by way of service, not by lording. Our model here is Christ himself: "The Son of Man did not come to be served but to serve" (Mt. 20:28). We see the actions and attitude of servanthood displayed many times in the life of Jesus—preeminently, when he washes the feet of the disciples (Jn. 13:12-17). Paul, echoing Jesus, tells the Corinthians that he does not "lord it over" their faith (2 Cor. 1:24).

3) Leaders have a responsibility to God. They do not own the flock: They are undershepherds, commissioned for the task of caring for it. They tend the flock in God's name (cf. Mt. 24:45).

3. The Christian and the State: Authority and Subordination in Politics.

Romans 13:1 is central to this topic: "Let everyone be subject to the governing authority .... He does not bear the sword in vain. They are God's ministers ...." The first question is whether the whole passage even refers to the state. It says to submit to the "powers," that is, some have thought, the "principalities and powers." But this interpretation does not make sense, because the passage talks about taxes. Rather, what Paul is referring to is the whole administrative powers governing a land, including tax collectors, police: everything from local minions to the emperor. All has been established by God. Paul speaks better of the dictatorial government of his day than Christians do of their elected governments today. Were it not for government, we would be at war with each other at all levels. It exists for our good. It is, as well, God's instrument for justice, including the administration of the death penalty.

Paul roots his theology of the state in the concept of Natural Law: The state exists to promote the general good, and to restrain evil. But the state is not absolute. It is limited by God's rule. This is, indeed, the kind of government which Christians can support: They place themselves under it knowing that it is under God.

The state is bound to higher standards which it cannot manipulate: good and evil. Those in authority are not a law unto themselves. Though they are not under the church, they are under God. The task of the state is to enforce the second tablet of the Decalogue. In the Old Testament, instructions for reform are always addressed to those in authority. And, throughout the Bible, encounters and confrontations with human authorities always take place under the assumption that God's authority creates standards which all are accountable to—for example, when John the Baptist confronts Herod over his adultery (Mk. 6:18). There are transcendent standards.

Absolute monarchies and totalitarian governments are bad because in them the law is embodied in one person. The prospect of God's judgement—both of ourselves and of those who rule—is the Christian basis for warning and confronting those who abuse their power (Heb. 9:27). But rulers are judged more severely (Lk. 12:48).

The relationship between the church and the state has always been a vexed one. Luther and Calvin espoused the doctrine of the two kingdoms. This view was in opposition to the Roman Catholic mingling of church and state and the Anabaptist withdrawal from the state. Luther and Calvin made a distinction: The church and the state are two separate kingdoms, but both are ruled by God. The state is responsible for the fostering of the creation order; the church, for the redemption order. The state uses the force, the church forgiveness. This scheme is based on the obvious truth that the same expectations can not be placed on both believers and non-believers. As well, it has something to do with appropriateness: The church should not be conducting police investigations; the state should not be forgiving seventy times seven. Under the state, evil is put down with the sword. Under the church, evil is overcome with good.

Calvin, in the *Institutes* IV, 20, spells out this distinction between the civil order and the church and explains that civil law is needed to restrain murder, theft and adultery. The reformational distinction of two kingdoms should not be confused with Augustine's distinction between the kingdom of heaven and the kingdom of this world. Rather, the reformers distinguished between two manners of divine rule: God rules the general creation through the state, and the redeemed creation through the church. Thus, the reformers divided ethics into social ethics and personal ethics.

There has been, throughout history, a deterioration of the two-kingdom doctrine, which has resulted from a misunderstanding of the phrase the "autonomy of the secular." By it, the reformers meant that the civil ruler was independent of the church. It did not mean, however, that he was independent of God. This phrase, and the reformer's insistence upon it, must be seen against the background of the battles between kings, emperors and popes. The reformers sought to free the state from ecclesiastical manipulation, but certainly not from divine rule and standards. Rather, the state was under a divine heteronomy, and was bound by the Decalogue. According to the reformational view, the church is under Christ, and the state is under God.

a) A Christian Response to Anarchism

The last two centuries have been marked, and marred, by political, moral and pedagogical anarchism. Michael Bakunin (1814-1876), in his *God and the State*, proposed that the abolition of law and order would create a brotherhood of love. He singled out Paul's pericope in Romans 13 for special scorn. Bakunin made a career out of anarchism; he was involved in revolutions in Berlin, Saxony, Italy and France. The 1871 Paris revolutionaries said of him—and the statement serves as a pronouncement on all anarchists—"It's great having a guy like him on the first day of the revolution, but on the second day, you have to abolish him."

Our century is one of lawlessness, and the philosophy and practice of anarchism is widespread. The Christian response is to acknowledge that the state imposes certain limitations on our freedom.

Admittedly, the state makes heavy demands on us. The state undoubtedly limits the individual's self-fulfilment and freedom. Nevertheless, Paul characterizes the government as good. Why? Because man's nature, being what it is, would destroy the freedom anarchism bestows. There is among us a lust for power and possessions that, allowed to breed unchecked, would mean that the law of the jungle would prevail. Power would make the new master. The anarchist is impossibly naive in his view of human nature: That nature, left to itself, tends toward good, not evil. Government, then, is God's provision for order in a fallen world, and it keeps man from tearing himself apart.

Religious anarchism is antinomianism. This is, not just a functional abrogation of the law, but the whole abrogation of it.

We must mention also in this context religious indifference and unconcern toward the state. Those groups with an otherworldly emphasis are not really concerned with the state's infringement on personal freedom: They simply do not want anything to do with the state. These groups order their life according to the Sermon on the Mount, and since this gives Christians an ethic which cannot be codified into civic law, they will have nothing to do with civil law. Instead, they focus on the church and have as little involvement as possible in the affairs of secular society. This issue is at the heart of the debate between the Magisterial and the Anabaptist wings of the Reformation. Calvin and Luther's response to the Anabaptist withdrawal from civil life was to point to the New Testament command that we respect authorities. Christians ought at least to be friends and counsellors of those in government.

b) Protestant Theology Limits the Authority of the State

Romans 13 speaks against both the degradation and the deification of the state. The state is subject to creation ordinances. Totalitarian demands by the state are therefore to be rejected by Christians. The limit of state authority is determined by the standards of good and evil reflected in the Ten Commandments. A government's legal power ends at the point where it commands the breaking of God's commands (Acts 5:27). A government goes beyond its authority when it calls good evil or evil good, when it demands absolute loyalty, or when it tries to convince or compel people not to be Christians. Any government which orders its citizens to transgress the second tablet of the Decalogue must be resisted.

Rank and file Christians have only the means of civil disobedience for resisting authorities: They are not to hand over the Holy Book, but they themselves cannot take action. "When they persecute you in this city," Jesus counselled his disciples, "flee to another." The Reformers, in keeping with this, advised emigration. Religious persecution is, after all, often local or regional.

The second level of resistance is the proper use of the office of preaching. The proper Christian response is, not the zealot armed with the gun, but the prophet armed with the word. Christianity aims to depose or reform the oppressive ruler, not to kill him. Resistance must be exercised by the weapon of language. This is why Luther did not support the peasant's war of 1525. Calvin also never accepted the right of regicide, the killing of the ruler: Even a tyrant must not be removed by murder. It is not fit for the church to issue a call to arms.

THE SIXTH COMMANDMENT

"You shall not murder."
(Ex. 20:17; Dt. 5:17)

A. Exposition

1. The Negative Version in the Old Testament

The Old Testament makes a distinction between manslaughter —unintentional killing—and murder—intentional killing. The Old Testament actually makes provision for "cities of refuge," places which harbour manslaughterers against the vengeance of a victim's relatives (eg., Dt. 19:1-13). Manslaughter, for example, would be killing someone by throwing a stone without looking. On the other hand, an intentional killing would involve premeditation, and is brought out in phrases such as "enmity" and "lying in wait" (see Num. 35: 9-34).

This commandment, then, is concerned with a specific kind of killing: intentional murder. J.J. Stamm, in *The Decalogue in Recent Old Testament Research*, points out the distinctive vocabulary of Exodus 20:13. The Hebrew word used in the sixth commandment is "rasah," which means an intentional killing. When Elijah makes his accusation against Ahab, he uses the word "rasah," a premeditated act (1 Kings 21:19; also, Jer. 7:9).

The commandment, however, does not rule out the death penalty. The commandment applies to individuals, not—and this is Luther's point—to government. The biblical basis for capital punishment is Genesis 9:5, 6, where death is the penalty for "blood spilled," and Romans 13:4, where Paul argues that the state wields "the sword" to punish the evildoer.

Capital punishment is an example of the talion formula: An eye for an eye, a tooth for a tooth. The punishment fits the crime. Critics today see it as barbaric. It is nothing of the sort. Rather, it is a measure of civilization: In ancient society, ruled by blood feuds, this put an end to spiralling acts of vengeance.

Neither does this commandment prohibit war. Warfare, while intentional, is not private.

2. The Negative Version in the New Testament

In Matthew 5:21, Jesus actually quotes Exodus 20:13 and radicalizes it: "Whoever is angry with his brother," he says, "will be subject to judgement." Scholars often call this pericope in Matthew the antithesis of the Sermon on the Mount. But the description is misleading. It implies that Jesus opposed the original commandments. The truth, though, is that Jesus' teaching was not antithetical to but a radicalization of the commandments. He surpassed, not cancelled, the original commandments. Calvin says that Christ is here condemning the murder, born of anger and bitterness, which takes place in the heart. Christ shifts the focus from the evil deed to the evil motive. He demands moral rightness, not merely legal correctness. The New Testament, in general, reinforces this teaching. 1 John 3:13, for example, says that anyone who hates his brother is a murderer. Paul, accordingly, includes hatred and anger in his lists of sins (see, for example, Gal. 5:20).

We have, through the refinement of manners, learned not to express hate. But what about our natural inclination to "think small" of someone? The sixth commandment, radicalized by Jesus, demands from us holiness in deed and in thought.

3. The Positive Version in the Old Testament

The teaching that murder is rooted in enmity, and that enmity itself is thus sinful, is not exclusive to the New Testament. The Old Testament, too, contains express commands against evil attitudes. Leviticus 19:7, for instance, reads, "You shall not hate your brother in your heart." An all-encompassing positive equivalent is "But you shall love your neighbor as yourself" (Lev. 19:18). The positive equivalent is to sustain life.

4. The Positive Version in the New Testament

Jesus connects obedience to God with the ethics of sustenance (see Mt. 25:31-46). This connection is reinforced in Christ's parables of stewardship: It is the believer's vocation to sustain God's people. The six corporal works of mercy in Matthew 25:31 ff also describe this ethos of sustenance, of preserving creation.

Jesus also summarizes this in Mark 3:4, where he equates doing good with saving life. Good is defined very much in physical terms. And sustenance here is not merely a matter of keeping life going; rather, it is active intervention to save life. Christian ethics involve us in attitudes and actions which can be compared to the work of a doctor, in contrast to, say, the work of a gardener. It is a medical, or causative, ethics. Its concern is not simply in maintaining health, but also in healing; not just in preserving life, but also in restoring it. The fulfilment of this ethic is beautifully illustrated in the parable of the Good Samaritan (Lk. 15).

This ethic is linked to Systematic Theology and the doctrine of God. The Lord is holy and makes holy. Paul speaks of the righteous one who makes righteous. Thus, the ethical impulse to help and heal is nurtured and guided by the very character and activity of God.

The ethics of healing relate also to human relationships. Relationships, like the people who engage in them, can be wounded, can be killed. But they can also be sustained and restored. This daring interpretation derives from Christ himself, both in his ministry and in his teaching. Jesus teaches, and shows, that the opposite of hatred—which is the root of murder—is to forgive (Mt. 5:23). The logic of this passage is that you can have no relationship with God if there is strife in your human relationships. This thought is put more starkly in 1 John 4:20: It is impossible to love God and hate your brother.

This principle is taught in many places in the New Testament. In the Lord's Prayer, for instance, the phrase "Forgive us our trespasses as we forgive those who trespass against us" indicates that the initiative for forgiveness resides with the Christian. Mark 11:25 reads, "Whenever you stand praying, if you hold anything against anyone, forgive him, so that your Father in heaven may forgive you your sins." The earthly process of forgiveness precedes the heavenly one. Christians must act out of a spirit of, not spitefulness, but forgiveness. Paul admonishes, "Do not let the sun go down on your anger" (Eph. 4:26). Anger accumulates into grudge and vendetta. Over time it takes on the proportions of murder. Paul, to guard against that, tells us to restore all relationships before evening. And, of course, the preeminent passage teaching forgiveness is Matthew 18:21 and 22, where Peter asks Christ if he should forgive "Up to seven times," and Christ responds that the times we forgive must be, in essence, unnumbered.

These passages which make God's willingness to forgive us hinge upon our willingness to forgive others speak, it appears, of a double justification: one based upon our profession of faith— our having been forgiven—and one based upon our life of faithfulness— our willingness to forgive. Certainly, the Christian is to imitate Christ in his willingness to forgive. We are to be agents of reconciliation. Both Christ, as he hung on the cross, and Stephen, as he fell before the barrage of hurled stones, demonstrated this ready willingness to forgive and be reconciled (Lk. 23:34; Acts 7:59). The parable of the Good Samaritan suggests that the Christian is to be an agent of reconciliation: the one who binds the wounds.

The New Testament also extends this call to care for and to nurture others to spiritual terms. And, again, the example derives from Christ. This is beautifully illustrated in Philippians 2, where Paul states, "Each of you should look not only to your own interests, but also to the interests of others" (2:4), and then, in verses 5-11, holds up Christ as our example for this. 1 Corinthians 10:24 lays down the principle of selflessness in even stronger terms: "Nobody should seek his own good, but the good of others."

The principle is, again, embodied in the parable of the Good Samaritan, who made the concerns of the other person his own. And this basic teaching is echoed in several other New Testament passages as well: "Love one another in brotherly affection" (Rom. 12:10); "Each of us should please his neighbor for his good, to build him up" (Rom. 15:2); "Welcome one another as Christ welcomed you" (Rom. 15:7). The consummation of this is love even for our enemies (Mt. 5:43).

B. Three Contemporary Issues: Abortion, Euthanasia and Suicide

1. Abortion

The Israelites would not have dreamt of abortion, specifically for three reasons: first, fruitfulness —the bearing of children— was commanded; second, they rejoiced in children. Children were considered a gracious gift from the Lord (Gen. 1:23); and, third, the Israelites lived by the promise that one of their children would be the Messiah. Abortion was virtually unknown in Jewry even as late as 1950.

In contrast to this Jewish abhorrence of abortion, both abortion and child-abandonment were widespread and largely accepted in the Roman world. Hippocrates' oath includes a promise not to perform or aid in the procurement of an abortion, and yet this did not appear to restrain the practice much. So, as the Gospel spread beyond Israel it had to deal with this issue (as well as issues such as homosexuality).

The earliest post-New Testament Christian moral instruction includes, "You shall not prepare poison or kill the newborn" (Didache 2:2). The preparation of poison may have been a technical term for abortion. The early church decided there was to be no penance for women who had an abortion. Later, this was changed to ten years of penance. Augustine allowed for abortion in medical emergency ("a necessary cruelty to kill the child in order to save the mother"), that is, in case of cross-breach.

At the level of the state, allowance must be made for abortion on medical grounds. Otherwise, the doctor is legally responsible for his medical decision. But the situation is different for Christians. A Christian may decide to commend the whole situation to prayer, knowing that "God works everything for good" (Rom. 8:28). And yet this attitude of faith cannot be presupposed for everyone.

Let us examine, in the light of Christian faith and ethics, some of the reasons often advanced for abortion. One of the main reasons is "therapeutic": cases where pregnancy coincides with certain diseases and the unborn child is sacrificed for the sake of the mother's life. Medical treatment and technology, however, have advanced to the point where this is rarely a necessity. All the same, legal allowance should be made for this circumstance.

In recent years, in the public battle, the term "therapeutic" has been stretched to include psychological problems. The argument is that the pregnant woman might, from psychological torment, commit suicide. This looser interpretation of "therapeutic" has opened a door to abuse in many countries. In Canada, for example, the authorities have often refused to define "therapeutic," and this has created a situation in which women can often seek therapeutic abortions for reasons of general distress. Some women do, indeed, experience "Pregnancy psychosis" during the first three months of pregnancy, but this is usually a passing phenomenon.

A second reason often given for abortion is eugenic—"good creation." This is where the child is expected to have mental or physical defects that will, according to the argument, impair the child's "quality of life." An example is when a mother contracts Rubella while pregnant, which may damage the child's vision or speech. But this is precarious ground upon which to justify abortion, for it is not at all certain that the child will have the expected defects. Abortion on these grounds comes very close to euthanasia. Who decides whether or not the person shall live? This is perhaps morally worse than infanticide—killing the child after birth—in that the abortion is done on the basis of potential defects.

Using eugenic arguments to justify abortion is often merely a ploy to disguise selfishness. Who is to say whether a child with defects has a lower quality of life than a child without defects? A case in point is children born to women who had taken the sedative Thalidomide—which often led to babies being born without arms or legs. A doctor who lived with Thalidomide children said they appeared to appreciate life more than other people.

A third reason given for abortion is rape. An American study shows that the majority of women who give this reason for an abortion never notified the police.

A fourth reason is social hardship—for example, where families already have many children and are living in poverty. But is it right that a child should be aborted because he or she might not be able to go to university? And even if it is a question of the child getting enough food to eat or clothes to wear, it is incredible that a society as affluent as our own should ever think of justifying abortion on social grounds. In Berlin, the bishop offered to pay for the education of children who would otherwise be aborted. Does the church elsewhere have the nerve and compassion to do likewise? In monasteries, a revolving wooden chest used to be built into the wall so that poverty-stricken mothers could leave their children to the care of the nuns. Perhaps it is a practice we should restore in some form.

For abortions on demand, the appointed-time-limit argument has been used. Dr. Morgenthaler, the Canadian abortionist, has taken a position close to this: that abortion on demand is morally permissible within a specified time limit—for example, the first three months of pregnancy. Or the decision to abort may be made by a committee of a doctor, a social worker, and one other. This is the current situation in Canada. In some other countries, an arbitrary limit of ninety days has been set. There is an ancient precedent lurking beyond this number: the ancient Aristotelian notion that a fetus is given a soul in thirty days if it is a boy and ninety days if it is a girl. In Greek thinking, life resides in personhood, in consciousness, in intellectual life. In Hebrew thinking, life is in the blood. Joseph Fletcher, the infamous founder of situation ethics, showed his greek-mindedness when he argued that it may be acceptable to kill children up to the age of two years because they do not demonstrate personality prior to that.

In 1967, the law against abortion was liberalized in England. It is interesting to observe the number of abortion clinics that emerged. There was the potential here for high economic return. Abortion became profitable. After two years, the British Medical Association reported a large number of bad situations. Cancer patients, for example, had been denied beds because abortion cases were thought to be more urgent.

In Canada, abortions are performed frequently in public hospitals. There were 4800 abortions in 1984 at Vancouver General Hospital in Vancouver, B.C., alone.

In several countries, doctors and nurses not willing to perform or assist in abortions have lost their jobs. A recent ad for the position of head doctor in Belgium read, "Catholics need not apply."

One of the many problems that arise from all of this is that of public financing: When the money we spend on health care does not go toward healing illness, why should the public feel obliged to pay for it? This may be an area for Christian civil disobedience.

The problem of abortion is related to the social and legal acceptance of common law marriage. But even the formerly sacred bounds of covenantal marriage have not remained inviolate to the issue of abortion: In 1976, the U.S. Supreme Court ruled that a married woman does not need her husband's permission to obtain an abortion. It is sad, and absurd, to consider that a married person is not legally permitted to sell jointly owned property without the other's consent, but a jointly conceived child can be disposed of apart from the decision of the father. The Supreme Court has even drafted laws that wedge themselves between families: A girl under 18 does not need her parents' consent for an abortion.

The church must speak with strength and clarity about the evil of abortion, but must speak, too, with gentleness and sensitivity to those who have had them. We need here a ministry of both warning and of comfort. And in girding up for the battle against abortion, it is poor strategy to go armed with only slogans. Careful and various distinctions must be made, and we must let love and compassion guide us. As the parable of the Good Samaritan (Lk. 15) teaches us, it is not enough to deplore the crime: We must be ready to risk our own comfort, spend our own money, to bring healing to those in distress.

2. Euthanasia

The morality of euthanasia—or "mercy killings"—has been debated since the 1890s. Before we enter the debate, it is important to distinguish three categories of euthanasia. The first can be defined as "to help in dying." This is the situation where the patient is in the final stages of life and gives his or her consent to their life being ended. The second category can be defined as "to help towards dying." This is the case where, though the last stage of life has not been entered, the patient sees no hope of recovery. A value judgement is involved. The third category is simply the termination of a life not considered worth living. This last can include, and has included, whole categories of people. The decision of the worthiness of the patient's life is usually made by doctors or government agents.

All three categories of euthanasia, however, have a shared philosophical basis: they all rest with a human decision about the worthiness of a particular life. And the problem with this is vividly illustrated in the Nazi's euthanasia program in Hitler's Germany. The Nazis, to decide whether a life was worth living, used many of the liberal bourgeois categories of "social usefulness" or "social fitness." On these grounds they planned to eradicate all mentally handicapped people and all epileptics—"useless mouths." Hundreds of thousands died on the zero-calorie diet.

The problem is precisely this: who decides, and on what criteria, what lives are worth living? What about invalid ex-drug addicts? What about seniors racked with senility? The truth is that no one is in a position to judge the value of human life, either another's or their own. We need, as Christians, to proclaim and practice compassionate concern for the elderly, the mentally handicapped, epileptics - for all people. Perhaps we would be less hasty to decide the value of human life on the basis of "usefulness" if we were to observe the many families who cherish a mentally or physically handicapped child. Such children restore to us the true nature of love: They are loved, not for their usefulness, but for their own sake, and that is how all love should be.

3. Suicide

Suicide was, in antiquity, part of the philosophy of the Stoics. The right to take one's own life was thought to ensure human freedom and dignity. More recently, humanists in Europe have been debating the "right" to kill oneself. A characteristic example is Jan Amery's book *The Right to My Own Death*. But both the

Stoic defense of suicide and the more recent ones spring out of a very narrow perspective of human life. Often suicide is an attempt to escape an unbearable situation. But the Christian believes that no situation is beyond the power of God to bring forgiveness and renewal.

Even Christians need to be reminded of this. Suicide occurs when there is a loss of vision, where there is no sense of purpose in life. Man appears to be built—to be designed—to live for a purpose: Just as an unused hand atrophies, so a life without purpose withers. Victor Frankl has argued that religion is almost necessary for this reason, because it gives man a sense of destiny, a shape and meaning to his life. It appears strange that the highest incidence of suicides are in affluent societies. But this, in fact, is not strange: The most affluent societies are also the most secularized, such as Sweden. We need a recovery of the idea of God's plan and meaning for life. In God's kingdom, there is no unemployment. Everyone has a place and a purpose.

A second common cause of suicide is loneliness. Here, too, secularism plays a key role, because it dissolves meaningful human community. This will always be the effect wherever self-fulfilment is made the highest human goal. Loneliness also marks out those with alcohol and drug addictions.

Christians need to work for the restoration of genuine friendship and fellowship. It is instructive that a recent report attributed the healing of homosexuals to the recovery among them of a goal in life and of fellowship. Christianity provides both. J. Adams has emphasized that preaching is preventative counselling. We can add that the family and Christian fellowship serve the same end.

THE SEVENTH COMMANDMENT

"You shall not commit adultery"
(Ex. 20:14; Dt. 5:18)

A. Exposition

With the seventh commandment, we enter again into a heated debate, judging by the precarious state of marriage in our society. Secularism chips away at the basis of marriage. On top of this, and connected with it, is the widespread social acceptance of common law marriages. The motto of today's society seems to be, "Stay single, take the pill."

1. The Negative Version in the Old Testament

The commandment against adultery is found in Exodus 20:14 and Deuteronomy 5:18. The holiness code also prohibits adultery (Lev. 20:10 ff). As well, this passage interprets the commandment by expanding its scope of reference: it also prohibits intercourse with a mother-in-law, homosexuality, bestiality (or sodomy with animals). These practices carry the death penalty. The passage prohibits some marriages as well.

Deuteronomy 22:22 also condemns adultery, but within a context that deals with the crime of rape. The Old Testament equates rape with assault and murder. But it also recognizes the possibility of a woman sharing in the guilt of rape: If a woman is raped in the city but fails to cry out for help, she is, with the man, equally responsible (Dt. 22:23-24; cf. 22:25-27).

The commandment, as we trace it through the Old Testament, also covers the psychology of adultery. Job 31:1 states, "I have made a covenant with my eyes not to look lustfully at a girl." And, a few verses further down, we have this: " ... if my heart has been led by my eyes" (v. 7). The heart, the seat of the will, is stirred to sin by the eyes. Admiration is one thing, but often it leads to fascination, to preoccupation, where one lies in wait to spy upon another. So, the psychological sequence in the Old Testament is this: first the look, then the thought, then preoccupation with the thought, and then the act. This psychological movement is strongly represented in the Proverbs, and it is illustrated by David's sin with Bathsheba (2 Sam. 12:11).

There is further material which interprets this commandment in the prophets: the parallel between love of God and married love (Hos. 2:19). From this analogy follows God's horror of divorce (Mal. 2:15b).

This is a good place to address the alleged laxity of the Old Testament on the issue of divorce. Deuteronomy 24:1 appears to allow a man to divorce his wife if she becomes "displeasing to him." But we need to examine the context here closely: Moses is dealing with, not so much the grounds for divorce, but the conditions for remarriage after successive divorces. Only by the worst exegetical mangling can this passage be made into a general absolution for divorce.

In the Old Testament, the occurrence of divorce is a fact but never a virtue. It is not part of creation: It is a consequence of the Fall. Furthermore, the analogy between marriage and the relationship between God and His people speaks of monogamy. God did not bind himself to many, but to Israel alone. The high value which the Old Testament placed on marriage is glimpsed in the custom of the bride-price, where the husband had to pay for the bride—for example, Jacob's 14 years of service to Laban for the right to marry Rachel (Gen. 29:16-30). Even in the case of rape, the price of the bride was 150 days of wages. And, though there are several examples of polygamy in the Old Testament, it was the exception—illustrated, for instance, in Nathan's parable to David about the poor man who had only one little ewe.

Finally, the Old Testament is very explicit about various sexual offenses: adultery, fornication, prostitution, bestiality, and homosexuality. Israel's strict sexual code was virtually unique in a world where pederasty (sex with young boys) and sacred prostitution were common practices. Freud thought that sexual motivation lay behind cultural achievement. Yet J.E. Unwin concluded that cultural achievement and sexual restriction and discipline go hand in hand (*Sex and Culture*, 1936). It is not surprising, then, that the cultural vigour of Israel was so great.

2. The Negative Version in the New Testament

John 7:53-8:11 contains the vivid and famous narrative of Christ's response to the woman caught in adultery. And although there is a textual problem with this passage—it is missing from the earliest extant manuscripts—its spirit and tone are nevertheless in keeping with what we know about Jesus. In this episode, some Pharisees and teachers of the law bring an adulteress to Jesus, saying, "The law of Moses commanded us to stone a woman caught in adultery. What do you say?" They pose for Jesus a shrewd legal dilemma. If Jesus says to spare her, he is in violation of Mosaic law. If he says to kill her, he violates Roman law. Christ at first remains silent, making only the curious gesture of writing on the ground with his finger. Yet the finger is the symbol of the Spirit of God, which wrote Scripture. Then, after their repeated questioning, he gives the magnificent reply, "If any of you is without sin, let him be the first to throw a stone at her" (v. 7b). After the crowd has slunk away in shamed silence, Jesus says to the woman that, though he does not condemn her, she is to "Go now and leave your life of sin" (v. 11b).

Even in forgiveness, Christ upholds the standard of the commandment. There is a beautiful principle here: Forgiveness abolishes, not the commandment, but its transgression. The forgiving Christ calls sin sin. But his forgiveness is the beginning place of the abolition of sin. The Mosaic commandment remains intact, but its penalty has been removed. "He [Christ] has abolished the curse of the law" (Gal. 3:13). Christ has shifted the commandment from a legal context to a moral one, from condemning to advising.

Jesus radicalizes the commandment in the Sermon on the Mount (Mt. 5:27-30; cf. Job 31:1). "Everyone," Jesus says, "who looks at a woman lustfully has already committed adultery with her in his heart" (v. 28). Christ's suggestion that the offender pluck his eyes out emphasizes the seriousness of the matter.

What are we to make of the harshness of this teaching? One thing that needs to be said is that there is a great difference between ethics, which deals with the potential sinner—and so with the question, "How are we to act ethically?"—and the ministry of restoration, which deals with the proven sinner—and so with the question, "What do we do now after we have acted unethically?" Leniency is misplaced if it is exercised in regard to ethics—that is, in regard to principles of conduct. Although gentle restorative measures are perhaps in order for those who have sinned, we need harsh preventative measures for those inclined to sin. This is especially true since our proneness to sin needs little or no outside enticement: It resides in our own hearts (Mt. 15:19). Transgression, we see once again, begins with the eyes—the heretics, Peter says, have eyes full of adultery (2 Pet. 2:14). Vigilance over our eyes has traditionally been the first guard against adultery. Luther says, for example, that seeing not only stirs lust for the moment, but sometimes haunts the memory, and so one may end up paying dearly for a simple unguarded moment, an initial leniency.

There is, though, a special responsibility for women. Luther felt that a woman encumbered with jewelry was signalling that her chastity was a burden. In our own day, we must be wary of much of women's fashions which are designed to entice.

The validity of the seventh commandment is presupposed in Jesus' prohibition of divorce. "Except for the case of unchastity ... everyone who marries a divorced woman commits adultery" (Mt. 5:32). Luke makes no exception: Neither the divorced man nor the divorced women should remarry, for by doing so they commit adultery (Lk. 16:18). The high seriousness with which Christ views this commandment informs the strictness of his teaching here.

But what are we to make of Matthew's exception clause (Mt. 19:9)? Luke and Mark (Mk. 10:11) do not have it. Matthew does not repeat it later, and its inclusion here is strange, since it indicates a leniency uncharacteristic of Matthew. We need to examine the passage more closely.

The word translated "unchastity" is the Greek word "porneia." This is a technical term for forbidden relations—that is, incestuous marriages. This is plausible since incest was common in Greece. The exception clause in Matthew 5, then, is best interpreted as referring to a forbidden relationship, presumably entered into prior to conversion to Christianity. So, Matthew is here allowing for the dissolution of a forbidden marriage. The same word is used in Acts 15:20. Here the context is the Jerusalem Council's decision to admit Gentiles to the fellowship on the condition that, among other things, they abstain from "sexual immorality" (porneia). We can conclude then that Matthew's exception clause is addressed to incestuous relationships. This is the only exegesis which doesn't leave gaping holes.

What about the "Pauline privilege" (1 Cor. 7:15): that a believer is not bound if the unbelieving spouse leaves? When we examine this passage, we see that Paul's concern is, not to find a loophole in a convert's marriage clause, but, rather, that faith should not be the cause of divorce. What Paul says is that, in the marriage between a Christian and non-Christian, if the non-believer wants a divorce, "Let it be so ... In such a case he is not bound" (1 Cor. 7:13-15). But he says nothing about whether either partner can remarry. In fact, that would contradict the earlier part of the passage.

The Pharisees in Jesus' time actively discussed the passage from Deuteronomy 24:1 which, according to them, permitted divorce "if a husband finds some indecency" with his wife. This is the background to the Pharisees' question to Jesus in Matthew 19:3: "Is it lawful for a man to divorce his wife for any and every reason?" For the Pharisees, the debate was over how loosely or narrowly to define the term "indecency." Rabbi Hillel broadened it to include a wife burning the dinner. But for Jesus—and this is evident in his response to the pharisees' question in Matthew 19—divorce is not an option.

Adultery is listed as one of the sins that exclude a person from the kingdom of God (1 Cor. 6:9-11). The passage condemns people who commit such sins, but it also holds out the promise of forgiveness. Paul uses the imperfect tense to speak of the finishedness of a believer's past sins: "so were some of you [adulterers, homosexuals, murderers, etc]." God's grace is life-changing. "If we walk in the light,"—that is, if we do not conceal our sin but confess it to God—"the blood of Jesus his Son cleanses us from all sin." The sin may be great, but the atonement is even greater.

3. The Positive Version in the Old Testament

The Old Testament does not contain much positive material concerning this commandment. We must remind ourselves, however, of the positive blessing which the seventh commandment protects: marriage. Just as life is defended by the sixth commandment—"Thou shall not murder"—so, too, marriage is being safeguarded in the seventh—"Thou shall not commit adultery." So the positive equivalent in the Old Testament is contained in its high view of marriage.

The first people were not simply male and female but a couple, with a mandate to "be fruitful and multiply" (Gen. 1:27, 28). One of the key purposes of marriage, then, is procreation. Yet marriage is richer than just this. God created it as well for fellowship and co-operation. "It is not good that man shall be alone," God says, "I will make him a helper similar to him." The word "helper" here is weighty. It means decisive and essential help. The same terminology often is used in reference to God as helper, for example in Psalm 70:5: "... come quickly to me, O God. You are my help ...."

Proverbs 31, a paean to the good wife, who is "more precious than jewels" (v. 10), gives us a portrait of the husband's "helper." The proverb pictures a wife of industriousness and productiveness, even though the husband almost seems to be retired. So the wife is hardly the husband's minion. Elsewhere in Scripture, examples of the love, courtship and honesty which are the biblical touchstones of good marriage abound (see, for eg., Gen. 24; 29:20; 1 Sam. 1:8). So marriage is designed for two purposes: for procreation, and for fellowship and co-operation in householding. In recognition of this, the Bible exempted newly married men from military service (Dt. 20:7; 24:5).

4. The Positive Version in the New Testament

Perhaps the most striking affirmation of marriage in the Bible is found in the extended analogy between marriage and the relationship of Christ to the church (Eph. 5:21-33). In this rich and intricate passage, Paul also enjoins that each man "love his wife as himself." In other words, the love that exists between man and wife is both analogous to the love that Christ has for his bride, the church, and an application of the commandment to love one's neighbour as one's self.

In some ways, the New Testament depicts marriage as a sacrament, "a reminder of the holy"; but marriage is never "a medium of the holy," because marriage needs forgiveness. The ideal is, again, for a couple to love one another as Christ loves the church. Christ extends, not just love to his people, but forgiveness as well. In the same way, forgiveness is central to the life of a marriage. "Forgive one another as Christ forgave you" (Eph. 4:32). Forgiveness is the simple secret of a lasting marriage. It sweeps away the little pebbles which, left untended, gather into a wall of separation.

The step after forgiveness is for each partner to make the other great, to lift him or her up to God, to assist, with loyalty and passion, in every way. For this task we proceed on, and are sustained by, the knowledge that we have been entrusted with one another. Each is a gift to the other. The crowning glory of marriage is when man and wife become co-workers, as with Priscilla and Aquila (Acts 18:2, 26; Rom. 16:2-4; 1 Cor. 16:19; 2 Tim. 4:19).

THE EIGHTH COMMANDMENT

"You shall not steal."
(Ex. 20:15; Dt. 5:19)

A. Exposition

1. The Negative Version in the Old Testament

Old Testament scholars think that the eighth commandment was originally against kidnapping. But here, in the Decalogue, the commandment is defined more narrowly: You shall not steal a man's possessions. The commandment was, however, interpreted more broadly in the Old Testament. In Genesis, even before the giving of the covenant at Sinai, the sin of theft is widened to include cheating: Jacob's cheating Esau of his blessing (Gen. 27:11), his cheating Laban of his flock (Gen. 30:25 ff), Laban's cheating Jacob (Gen. 29:23 ff). The commandment is also interpreted there in a more strict sense—such as when Joseph, to tests his brothers' integrity, places his silver cup in Benjamin's sack (Gen. 44). The penalty for such theft is death (Gen. 44:9). Joseph's abduction, or kidnapping, by his brothers is also a form of theft.

The commandment is repeated in both the holiness code and the Book of Covenant. The history of the interpretation of this commandment follows Luther in its broadness. False dealing is theft (Ex. 23:1). Taking economic advantage of someone who is weak is oppression and robbery (Dt. 24:15).

Exodus 22: 1, 4, 7 give the terms of restitution: double repayment where the stolen goods are recoverable; four- or fivefold return where the stolen goods are not recoverable. This principle lies behind David's response to Nathan's parable—that the man who has stolen and killed the poor man's sheep must pay back four times over (2 Sam. 12: 5, 6). If the thief could not make restitution he was to be sold into slavery.

The commandment against theft, though interpreted broadly, also had precise stipulations which limited it. Deuteronomy 23:24, for example, makes allowance for eating grapes off the vine in a neighbour's vineyard, but prohibits the gathering of the fruit.

Further interpretive material on the eighth commandment is found in the prophets. In general, the prophets enlarge on this commandment. Hosea links theft with a lack of faithfulness, love and knowledge of God (Hos. 4:2-6). Isaiah warns against the exploitation of widows and orphans (Isa. 10:1-3). Amos elaborates on the ethical demands imposed by the command by speaking against the evil machinations in the business world which amount to theft (Amos 8:4-6).

The theme of theft wrought through conniving business practice is a recurring one in the Old Testament. Leviticus 25:14 commands that "There shall be no wrong-doing in trading." Proverbs 11:26 speaks of the curse on one who withholds grain in time of need in order to force prices up. The temptations to deceitfulness are especially strong for those in business. And yet, though "Bread gained by deceit seems sweet," in the end it is like gravel in the mouth (Prov. 20:17).

2. The Negative Version in the New Testament

The sin of theft occurs in the sin lists of the New Testament (Mt. 15:19; 1 Cor. 6:9). "Thieves will not inherit the kingdom of God." Christ condemns the Pharisees because they are, among other things, full of extortion (Mt. 23:25). 1 Peter 4:15 and 1 Thessalonians 4:6 warn against theft and deception. Ephesians 4:28 is the classic New Testament passage, because here Paul both admonishes against stealing and exhorts toward honest work: The passage fuses the negative and the positive aspects of the commandment.

Motivation in the Old and New Testaments

The root of theft lies in covetousness and greed, and so it is difficult to distinguish, at the level of motivation, the eighth commandment from the tenth: The forces in man which tempt him to break this commandment are themselves condemned in the tenth commandment. And yet, this intertwining of commandments should not surprise us, for the commandments speak to man, not in fragments, but in their entirety, their togetherness. They reinforce one another. In a similar way, Proverbs 10:3b says that a man who is greedy for gain curses the Lord. This shows the close connection between the sins dealt with in the first, the second, the eighth and the tenth commandments. So, when speaking on theft special attention must be paid to the question of motivation.

Jesus condemns avarice. Luke 12:15 contains one of Christ's stern warnings against greediness, and then he gives an example of greed in the parable of the rich man and his barn, a parable of the folly of hoarding and miserliness. Jesus includes greed among the list of sins (Mk. 7:22), and Paul names it as one of the sins that excludes a person from the kingdom (1 Cor. 6:10). In Ephesians 5:5 and Colossians 3:5, greed is equated with idolatry. Both passages also closely link sexual sin with greed. There could be a subtle but telling anthropological statement here: That lust and the lust for money have an intimate relation. Perhaps both, too, are manifestations of possessiveness.

In James 5:1-6 the affluent are accused of hoarding and exploitation of the labourer. The strong suggestion is that greed is at the root of what the wealthy do. The New Testament sums up the matter in 1 Timothy 6:10: "The love of money is the root of all evils." Pursuit of wealth soon becomes all-consuming: Judas' life preeminently illustrates that sad truth.

The cure lies in being satisfied with sufficiency. We need to suppress the passion for more, to be glad with what is adequate for our needs. The desire for more is, like the cracked jug, always needing filling and never full.

3. The Positive Version in the Old Testament

The positive equivalent to greed is generosity. An example of this from the Old Testament is found in Genesis 14:14-26, where Abraham liberates Lot from marauders and restores to him his possessions. The story is made memorable by Abraham's own refusal to share in the bounty, to take even a fair portion of the recovered booty: Abraham's jealousy for his God is such that he wants no man to be able to say that he made Abraham rich.

The Bible does not condemn wealth. But it makes it clear that there are duties that flow from wealth. There is *Noblesse oblige*: "Nobility has its obligations." We might change that to *Richesse oblige*. The Old Testament delineates such obligations: almsgiving, leaving the harvest gleanings for the poor. Proverbs 19:17 even equates kindness to the poor with lending to the Lord. The Hebrew word for almsgiving, in the plural, indicates that the act is the very embodiment of righteousness.

Beyond almsgiving is the Old Testament injunction to tithe (Mal. 3:8). Tithing is to be for the Lord (Num. 18:21-24). Every third year the tithe was to be given to the poor (Dt. 26:12; 14:28). So here again charity enters into the motive for generosity. In Leviticus 25, the famous chapter of Israel's social ethics and of the year of Jubilee, we read: "If your brother becomes poor then you shall sustain him."

4. The Positive Version in the New Testament

Ephesians 4:28 is a brilliant application of ethics: "Let the one who steals no longer steal but let him work so that he may give to the poor." There is, in this brief verse, a threefold sequence of reform. First, the thief is to desist from his thieving. Second, he is, as a positive alternative to theft, to work. And third, he is to give to the poor. The passage sketches out the transformation from parasite to provider. This captures the New Testament emphasis on self-support. Diligence and industriousness are good witnesses to outsiders, and they allow for generosity in giving (2 Thess. 3:11-12). So the New Testament replaces theft with thrift and greed with giving. Instead of covetousness, charity (Rom. 12:8).

John the Baptist says that the man with two coats should share with the man who has none (Lk. 3:11). James 2:14-17 suggests that the sharing of material gifts is training for and an expression of the sharing of spiritual gifts (cf. Rom. 1:11; 1 Thess. 2:8). This theme is vividly applied in Matthew 25:25 ff, the passage which contains the six works of mercy: feed the hungry, give water to the thirsty, welcome strangers, clothe the naked, visit the sick and the imprisoned. These, all acts of sharing, are the touchstones of true discipleship (cf. the famous passage in the Old Testament, Isa. 58). All six acts speak of sustaining the life in need.

The Christian virtue of sharing was institutionalized in the early church (see Acts 4:32-35). The early church also practised transcontinental sharing (2 Cor. 8-9; Heb. 6). The concept of economic equality—the giving out of one's abundance to make up for another's lack (see 2 Cor. 8:14)—is interesting. It reflects a spiritual truth: God has invested gifts in us so that we might benefit those in need. This truth is made plain in the parable of the talents (Mt. 25:14-30), which can be read at both a spiritual and a material level. All God gives us—money, gifts, possessions—are talents with which he entrusts us. In the parable, the faithful servant is the one who invests the gift. The one who hoards it is considered wicked.

The spiritual form of giving is especially emphasized in Philippians 2:3, 4. We are to look out for the interests of others and in this, as Philippians 2:6 says, have the "same mind as Christ." We are to imitate Christ, and Christ came to give himself, and to give us life: "The thief comes only to steal, I have come that they may have life" (Jn. 10:10). It was, preeminently, Christ's example which shaped and fixed the attitude of the early Christians toward giving and sharing. "It is more blessed to give than receive" (Acts 20:35).

B. Reformational and Contemporary Exposition on the Eighth Commandment

Luther warns against interpreting this commandment too narrowly. He includes under the category of theft servants who neglect their duties and the attitude of negligent workers. Masters also often transgress this law, giving less than is due. Luther condemns those who rob publicly. Their theft is done openly and yet it goes unpunished. His criticism thus takes in the whole business world. In his pamphlet *On Trade and Usury* (1524), Luther defends the doctrine of the just price. He recommends that businessmen think of themselves as salaried employees of the Lord.

Luther's concept is a Christian alternative to the law of supply and demand. It stands against that ironclad law of capitalism. Calvin, reinforcing Luther, says that those who raise the price of grain in time of famine commit semi-homicide.

Luther also included under theft sins of omission: If you fail to help someone who is without shoes or food, you steal from him. In a way this echoes the earlier teaching of Chrysostom when he said that your goods are not your own, but simply entrusted to you. "The earth is the Lord's," and God's people are proprietors. They are hereditary tenants, merely keeping the land.

Theft has become acceptable in a number of areas in contemporary society. Many think nothing of pilfering office supplies, or of pretending illness and receiving sick pay. There is widespread cheating in unemployment and medical insurance claims. Many yield to the strong temptation not to declare goods brought across the border. And tax fraud is rife. There is a popular European slogan that captures the essence of this thinking: "Earn your money in Germany and live in Liechtenstein." The unfairness of this attitude is plain: People who cheat on taxes still use bridges and streets and libraries—those things built and maintained through tax money. The paying of taxes is a fundamental obligation of those who benefit from society, and Christians especially, who are commanded by God to live upright and conscientious lives, must pay their taxes.

THE NINTH COMMANDMENT

"You shall not give false testimony against your neighbor."
(Ex. 20:16; also Dt. 5:20)

[Dr. Klaus Bockmuehl never taught a class about the ninth commandment. This text was compiled by Elisabeth Bockmuehl.]

The place, or "Sitz Im Leben" of this commandment is obviously the lawcourt, and that defines the similarity between the third and the ninth commandment.

A. Exposition

1. The Negative Version in the Old Testament

In dealing with the third commandment, we talked about the misuse of an oath in connection with the name of God in court. The misuse of the oath could be dealt with in connection with the ninth commandment, i.e. false testimony against a neighbor. On the first table (third commandment) the Decalogue attends to the majesty of the divine name. On the second tablet it is a matter of avoiding damage to the name of a neighbor.

In his 11th sermon on the Ten Commandments Calvin tells us, concerning Deuteronomy 5:20, that as far as we speak the truth, we support our neighbor's honor. In the same sermon Calvin talks about the instrument of the tongue: a small muscle, that can light a fire (compare Jas. 3:1-11). God gave us a tongue, so that we can express our love for one another. Therefore we should not misuse our tongue by gossiping against each other. Gossip transforms the gift of language into a poison. Job uses the phrase of "the lash of the tongue" (Job 5:21). The typical example of a false testimony is of course Mark 14:55-56 during the trial of Jesus, where it says, "Many testified falsely against him."

Often, we are requested to judge one another. In doing so, it is easy to give information which is not one hundred percent correct. A word of rabbinic wisdom literature says: Nasty talk and slander kills all three people involved: the person one talks about, the speaker and the eager listener! Slander leads to the breakdown of every community. Therefore the law of holiness recommends, "Do not go about spreading slander among your people ... but love your neighbor as yourself, I am the LORD" (Lev. 19:16, 18).

The Codex Hammurabi says (compare Dt. 19:16-21): "If a man informs against another and declares him a murderer, but he is not found guilty of murder, the accuser should be punished with the death penalty."

But what should one do, if one does have a complaint against one's neighbor? Certainly one should not spread slander to a third person, but one should talk to the other face to face. If this fails, one can act in the way recorded in Matthew 18:15-16: Try to resolve your dispute in the presence of two witnesses. If this does not solve the problem, "... tell it to the church; and if he refuses to listen even to the church, treat him as you would a pagan or a tax collector" (Mt. 18:17). In the midst of this, it remains important to distinguish between the person and the point of controversy.

2. The Positive Version in the New Testament

One could describe this commandment in a positive way as follows: You shall give a true testimony about and for your neighbor. In Ephesians 4:25 we find the positive fulfilment of this commandment: "Therefore each of you must put off falsehood and speak truthfully to his neighbor, for we are all members of one body." And in Colossians 3:9-10 we read:

> *"Do not lie to each other, since you have taken off your old self with its practices and have put on the new self, which is being renewed in knowledge in the image of its Creator."*

So we can say that the ninth commandment does not only deal with the verbal transgression of the commandment, but it addresses the truth of human life altogether. Christ is the truth, and this is the basis for our salvation and for our life. The ninth commandment speaks about the identity of man in the presence of God and in front of our fellow-men (compare: Jan M. Lochmann, *Wegweisung und Freiheit*, Gütersloh (1984), p. 130).

B. The Interpretation of the Ninth Commandment in the Catechisms

In Martin Luther's *Small Catechism* we find about the eighth (ref. ninth) commandment:

"What does this mean? Answer: We should fear and love God, and so we should not tell lies about our neighbor, nor betray, slander, or defame him, but should apologize for him, speak well of him, and interpret charitably all that he does" (Tappert, p. 343).

In the *Large Catechism* Luther says about this commandment:

"The right way to deal with this matter would be to observe the order laid down by the Gospel ... where Christ says: 'If your brother sins against you, go and tell him his fault, between you and him alone.' Here you have a fine, precious precept for governing the tongue which ought to be carefully noted if we are to avoid this detestable abuse. ... Likewise, if someone should whisper to you what this or that person has done, teach him, if he saw the wrongdoing, to go and reprove the man personally, otherwise to hold his tongue" (Tappert, p. 402).

The *Heidelberg Catechism* answers question number 112:

"What is God's will for us in the ninth commandment? Answer: God's will is that I never give false testimony against anyone, twist no one's words, not gossip or slander, nor join in condemning anyone without a hearing or without a just cause. Rather, in court and everywhere else, I should avoid lying and deceit of every kind; these are devices the devil himself uses, and they would call down on me God's intense anger. I should love the truth, speak it candidly, and openly acknowledge it. And I should do what I can to guard and advance my neighbor's good name."

THE TENTH COMMANDMENT

"You shall not covet your neighbor's house. You shall not covet your neighbour's wife, or his manservant or maidservant, his ox or donkey, or anything that belongs to your neighbour."
(Ex. 20:17; also Dt. 5:21)

A. Exposition

1. The Negative Version in the Old Testament

The principal texts are Exodus 20:17 and Deuteronomy 5:21. There is an obvious connection between this commandment and the eighth, the commandment against theft. The new element here is that of motive, of thought: the eighth commandment condemns the external act, the tenth the wrong desire in which theft is rooted. The Hebrew word for covet is the verb "chamad" and "awah", which connote a strong desire and possessiveness. It is the same verb used in Psalm 106:14, which describes a desperate longing of the Israelites. 1 Kings 21 provides another vivid example, where Ahab craves Naboth's vineyard. The word is used also in 2 Samuel 23:15 to describe David's longing for water: In order to obtain it, his men had to risk their lives.

Deuteronomy 7:25 warns against a particular form of covetousness. The Israelites are told not to "covet the silver or gold" which is on the Canaanite gods being destroyed by fire. And Joshua 7:21 gives a concrete illustration of it in the theft of Achan. Achan, describing the sequence leading up to his taking some of the Babylonian plunder, says "When I saw, I coveted, then I took." The psychology of covetousness and theft is similar to that which we saw in adultery, a similarity reinforced in Proverbs 6:25, where the word covet is used to describe lust. Covetousness has erotic connotations.

2. The Negative Version in the New Testament

Christ, again, radicalizes the commandment (Mt. 5:28). Here, Christ warns against looking "at a woman greedily." Here again we see the link between lust and greed.

There is something in the human heart that inclines it toward evil. Dark desire—covetousness—is at the root of most sin. In this way, this last commandment is representative of the entire Decalogue. "What causes fights and quarrels among you?" James asks. "Don't they come from your desires that battle within you? You want something but don't get it. You kill and covet, but you cannot have what you want ...." (Jas. 4:1-2).

Luther takes all these things into consideration. In the *Large Catechism* he lists a number of ways we violate this commandment. He claims there is hardly a civil law case which does not transgress this commandment.

James 4:2 speaks of the acquisitive bent in human nature. Psychologists, only recently discovering what the Bible taught long ago, speak of the developmental stage in children where they want to swallow everything, acquire everything, consume it all. We never really shed this possessive instinct: it only takes more subtle and sophisticated forms.

One way this acquisitiveness manifests itself is in our actual dissatisfaction with possessions. It's not the having but the getting we like. Just as accelerating is more thrilling than merely going fast, so getting a thing is, for us, better than having it. In some economic theories, coveting has been made into a virtue. Such theories reflect the larger pattern and movement of our society, where those things in ourselves we once tried to purge we now enshrine.

What is behind this commandment not to covet? It is directed against the human habit of rooting identity in possessions. "I have, therefore I am." The depth of this habit is seen in Adam and Eve, who, though they had been given extravagant abundance, desired that which had been forbidden. Covetousness is desire which is not limited to human needs.

3. The Positive Version in the Old Testament

The material is sparse. Generally, the Old Testament presents work and sharing as positive alternatives to acquisitiveness. This is especially pronounced in the Proverbs. Proverbs 13:4, for example, says that "The soul of the sluggard slaves, while the soul of the diligent is made rich." And Proverbs 21:25 says that "The hands of the sluggard refuses to labour." The repeated emphasis is on industriousness.

4. The Positive Version in the New Testament

The New Testament stresses the attitude of contentedness and modesty: "If we have food and clothing we should be content, for we brought nothing into the world" (1 Tim. 6:6-10). There almost seems to be an echo here of Matthew 25 and Christ's command to give water to the thirsty, clothes to the naked, friendship to the outcast. There, too, the emphasis is on the basic necessities of living. Hebrews 13:5 tells us to "be content with what you have." This echoes Matthew 6:32, which adds to the injunction to contentment a warning against the faithlessness of craving and anxiety: Faith in God's provision banishes anxiety. Material possessions are to be at our service, not we at theirs.

Paul, in his farewell address to the Ephesian elders, declares "I have not coveted ... but these hands ministered to my necessities and those with me" (Acts 20:33, 34). The distinction between necessities and superfluities recurs continually in the New Testament. Paul adds in his farewell address that "by so toiling one must sustain the weak," and then reminds his listeners of Christ's principle that it "is more blessed to give than receive" (Acts 20:35). So here he has outlined the New Testament attitude to material goods: first, we are not to covet; second, we are to work for our necessities; and third, we are to give to the needy and the weak.

A second alternative to greed and anxiety in the New Testament is prayer. James says bluntly, "You do not have because you do not ask ... You spend it for your ends ..." (Jas. 4:3). James is echoing here the Sermon on the Mount: "Ask and it will be given to you, for everyone who asks will receive" (Mt. 7:7). The alternative to craving is to ask God.

The third alternative is a positive form of yearning and anxiety: the passionate pursuit of the Kingdom of God. Jesus, in Matthew 6:33, tells his followers to "seek first the kingdom of God and his righteousness." Here is one place where craving, where passionate desire, is blessed. Colossians 3:1-2 encourages to set both our hearts and our minds on things above. In this context, it is interesting to examine Matthew 11:12, where Christ says that "The kingdom of heaven has been coming violently, and violent men lay hold of it." The Kingdom is the one possession for which our desire should be vigourous, violent. Jesus himself appeared to feel this way: "I have come to send fire on the earth and how I wish it were already kindled" (Lk.12:49).

Indeed, that might summarize the teachings of the entire Ten Commandments: that we are to pursue the Kingdom with a fiery zeal and a passionate desire. For the commandments in their totality teach what Christ taught were the greatest commandments: to love the Lord our God with all our heart and soul and strength, and to love our neighbour as ourself.

THE TEN COMMANDMENTS: ARE THEY STILL VALID?

Are the Ten Commandments still valid for us today? Are they valid only for Christians, or for all people? Or are they perhaps only for Jews and pagans, but not for Christians? And is it merely piety or the inertia of conservatism that keeps them in our catechism, in the doctrinal strong-room of the church? Are they still with us simply because no one has dared to question the ancient moral habits of the church? Wouldn't a business, eager to rationalize for the sake of success, have long ago cleared them to a museum of ancient Near East?

Some prominent speakers in the church have come to just this conclusion and caught the headlines with it. One, a German church president, stated that it was impossible to prescribe a catalogue of eternal norms of conduct; rather, the Christian was to decide in the given situation what love would command him or her to do. Therefore, when it came to personal ethics, the Decalogue was out of the question. On another occasion this same man said that it was equally impossible in a pluralistic society to accept the Ten Commandments as the basis for social morality and the law of the state—something most countries took for granted until very recently.

Another Protestant ethicist, with earned doctorates in theology and sociology, brought his sociological thinking to bear on the Decalogue. Calling the Ten Commandments "those ancient norms" and "a nomad law," he relativized them historically and sociologically. The civilized world of the industrial age was too far removed from the world of the Ten Commandments: They could hardly help us, let alone be authoritative. They were, rather, a hindrance to modern life.

According to at least two theologians, then—to put it in terms used during the Reformation—the Decalogue belongs neither to the pulpit nor to the town hall. Where then does it belong? Merely to the history of Israel? How shall we answer these two suggestions? Should we agree with one or the other, and if not, why not? Why does the church continue to preach the Ten Commandments? To whom are the Ten Commandments given?

I shall try to answer these questions with three theses: 1) the Ten Commandments obligate the people of God to whom they are given; 2) the Ten Commandments recommend themselves to every person as an appropriate definition of the good; 3) the Ten Commandments are the framework of Christian ethics; they need to be filled with love, by the guidance of God's Spirit.

Is the Decalogue valid today, and for whom? It is indeed still necessary to ask these questions. While studying the Bible, it is of primary importance to take notice of the circumstances and context of the text. For example, consider this introduction to the commandments

"And now, O Israel, give heed to the statutes and the ordinances which I teach you, and do them; that you may live, and go in and take possession of the land which the LORD, the God of your fathers, gives you. You shall not add to the word which I command you, nor take from it; that you may keep the commandments of the LORD your God which I command you." (Dt. 4:1-2).

To whom is this appeal of Moses directed? To "Israel," of course, and more exactly to a certain generation in the history of the people of Israel - those who came out of Egypt. The Exodus is the original historical setting of the Ten Commandments.

But is that single generation the only one to whom the Decalogue is addressed? Already at Mt. Sinai, questions about the general and timeless applicability of these words were raised —the first precedent for similar questions asked today:

"When your sons ask you in time to come, 'What is the meaning of the testimonies and the statutes and the ordinances which the LORD our God has commanded you?'" (Deut. 6:20).

"The Lord *our* God" - that the Lord of the Decalogue is our God is accepted. But as to the commandments, we hear the little note of dissociation, as verses 21-25 go on to say, "which the Lord has commanded *you*." This second generation was already being told that the commandments were binding on all generations of Israel, every living generation, because they all belong together as a "corporate personality."

The Decalogue, then, is addressed to Israel, meaning this distinctive *nation* which has come from Egypt. The introduction to the actual text of the decalogue makes this point: "I am the LORD your God, who brought you out of the land of Egypt, out of the house of bondage" (Ex. 20:2).

And in Deuteronomy, the peculiar and unique character of Israel is unmistakably expressed:

> *"Or has any god ever attempted to go and take a nation for himself from the midst of another nation, by trials, by signs, by wonders, and by war, by mighty hand and an outstreched arm, and by great terrors, according to all that the LORD your God did for you in Egypt before your eyes?"* (Dt. 4:34).

Therefore, the answer must clearly be "No, the Decalogue is not just addressed to a single generation." Israel is a special case. They are God's covenant people, and the Ten Commandments, as has been shown by Old Testament scholars, are the basic law and constitution of this covenant.

In his teaching on the Decalogue and in general, Martin Luther stressed the importance of discerning to whom a biblical text is addressed, and especially "whether it means you." Concerning the Ten Commandments, he said: "From the text we clearly see that the Ten Commandments (as such) do not concern us. Because God has not brought us from Egypt, but only the Jews" (mentioned in his sermon of August 27, 1525, "Instruction on how Christians are to apply Moses"). Consequently, the law of Moses does not bind the Gentiles—it has no authority for non-Jews.

Such startling conclusions raise a number of questions: How then does the Decalogue get into Luther's small and large catechism, and so into the confessional writings of the Lutheran Church? And why would Luther himself have expounded the Decalogue, through preaching and print, more than a dozen times during his lifetime? How then does the Decalogue get into the Christian church and pulpit? There are several answers to these questions.

First, although Christians do not belong to Israel in a biological sense, yet from the perspective of the history of salvation Christians are included in the "new covenant," are members of the one people of God: "That in Christ Jesus the blessing of Abraham might come upon the Gentiles" (Gal. 3:14).

In another place, Paul makes the same point with an illustration which must have been as much a paradox to him as it still is to us: "But if some of the branches were broken off, and you, a wild olive shoot, were grafted in their place to share the richness of the olive tree" (Rom. 11:17).

If this is true, then we should ask not whether the Ten Commandments are valid for us today, but rather how could the Christian church ever legitimately drop them? One of the former generation of Swiss Reformed theologians, one-time Professor of Ethics in the University of Berne, Alfred de Quervain, therefore concluded rightly: "As we for Christ's sake and through the gift of the Holy Spirit have become members of this people, and as these commandments make known God's will for all sanctified—they also bind us. Christ has not come to abolish the commandments, but to fulfill them" (*Die Heiligung*, 1946, p. 248).

Second, it is by the authority of Christ that the Ten Commandments are valid for all who follow him. Moses is an authority for Christians insofar as Jesus took up his teaching. Jesus took the Ten Commandments seriously, unconditionally. In his meeting with the rich young ruler (Mt. 19:18), he quoted them as the basic instruction for the way to eternal life. He submitted to the Decalogue when he contrasted God's commandments to the traditions of the elders (Mt. 15:2). Part of his Sermon on the Mount is based on commandments from the Decalogue; his own new teaching is a heightening, an intensification of the Decalogue's commandments and not, as is often said, an antithesis to them. (The *wording* of the Sermon on the Mount—"you have heard that it was said...But I tell you..."—is antithetical, but there is radicalization of the commandments, not antithesis, in the *content* of what Jesus says.)

Jesus warned his listeners not to misconstrue what he intended, something which could easily happen when no distinction is made between God's commandments and human moral traditions. "Think not that I have come to abolish the law and the prophets," Jesus said, "*I have come not to abolish them but to fulfill them*" (Mt. 5:17).

In his actions, too, Jesus is true to the commandments. His much-debated actions on the Sabbath are no exception. If there is to be no contradiction between Jesus' words and his actions, then his deeds on the Sabbath have to be understood not as the abolition, but as the fulfilment of the Sabbath commandment. For Jesus said:

> *"For truly, I say to you, till heaven and earth pass away, not an iota, not a dot, will pass from the law until all is accomplished. Whoever then relaxes one of the least of these commandments and teaches men so, shall be called least in the kingdom of heaven: but he who does them and teaches them shall shall be called great in the kingdom of heaven. For I tell you, unless your righteousness exceeds that of the scribes and the Pharisees, you will never enter the kingdom of heaven"* (Mt. 5:18-20).

This righteousness that exceeds that of the Pharisees is the righteousness given to us freely by God. Jesus makes this clear when he rebukes the scribes and Pharisees for teaching harsh laws but never living up to them themselves (Mt. 23:1-4). This righteousness, though freely given by God, must be realized in the sentiments of our hearts as well as in our actual deeds—keeping the commandments and doing the things the Spirit teaches us which by far surpass the law. For those, then, who according to the "great commission' have been taught to obey everything he commanded his apostles, the Ten Commandments remain in force "till heaven and earth pass away."

That the apostles repeated the commandments in the letters of the early church, and that the church as a matter of course continued to single out a special day of the week, witness the validity of the Decalogue for the Christian church. The Lord God of Israel is the Father of Jesus Christ. His character, his sanctity and righteousness will not change. By reason of the authority of Christ, the Ten Commandments are valid for the people of God, today as much as when they were first given. They are the framework, the basis for God's communion with his people. Observing them spells blessing, transgressing them brings the curse of the Eternal.

Concerning the Ten Commandments, Karl Barth wrote:

> *"The Decalogue...is...in fact the basic event in the story of Israel - it unfolds the programme of the whole history of this people...and therefore by implication of His elect community ...the Church. It was*

not, therefore, without justification that the Decalogue was adopted as the basis of the Christian catechism. It is the foundation-statute of the divine covenant of grace and valid for all ages. Everything that the true God, the Founder and Lord of this covenant, has commanded and forbidden, or will command and forbid, is to be found within the framework of the programme of all His decisions and purposes as contained in the Decalogue" (Church Dogmatics, vol. II/2, p. 685).

The third reason for retaining the Decalogue in the teaching of the church is that it is the best comprehensive description of the Natural Law concept which binds all people. This is the theme of my second thesis.

If, as we have seen, the Decalogue is given particularly to the people of God, what does it say to people in general? We find an answer in Deuteronomy 4:6:

"Keep them and do them; for that will be your wisdom and your understanding in the sight of the peoples, who, when they hear all these statutes, will say, 'Surely this great nation is a wise and understanding people.'"

The Decalogue is described as the special property and priviledge of Israel, something which they will contribute to the family of nations. It is assessed as being especially wise and worthy of praise by all nations. This verse indicates that these commandments will be considered astonishingly judicious and sensible by every nation; everyone will reckon them to be a standard definition of the good. Throughout history their value has been discovered and rediscovered again and again. Something has been revealed to the people of Israel with which all nations agree. For all people strive after justice, and the Ten Commandments have proved to be an apt definition of it.

The apostle Paul expressed the same insight and experience in a more doctrinal manner:

"When Gentiles who have not the law do by nature what the law requires, they are a law unto themselves, even though they do not have the law. They show that what the law requires is written on their hearts, while their conscience also bears witness and their conflicting thoughts accuse or perhaps excuse them". (Rom. 2:14-15).

To every person the consciousness of good and evil is given so as to make them realize and acknowledge the Ten Commandments as the definition of the good.

Precisely from Romans 2:14-15, therefore, Luther argued for the validity of the Decalogue for non-Christians as well as for Christians: "For what God has given to the Jews through Moses, he has also written into the hearts of all men: Moses is consonant with nature" (Luther, in his afore-mentioned sermon). The mute moral consciousness within every person finds its proper expression in (at least) the so-called second tablet of the Mosaic Decalogue.

Romans 2:14-15, thus, is the source of the acceptance within the Christian tradition of the idea of Natural Law. This concept, central to the exposition of Christian ethics for centuries, has come under strong attack only in the last two generations. Karl Barth's *Gospel and Law* (1935) is a milestone on the route to the rejection of Natural Law as a category of ethics. Even in Roman Catholic moral theology which, unlike Protestant ethics, is built thoroughly on the notion of Natural Law, the concept is being disputed. But while Catholic theologians are moving away from the concept of Natural Law, due at least in part to the demand for situation ethics (the very opposite to an eternal, Natural Law), within Protestant ethics there are traces today of an reconsideration of the concept. It may be recovered as an indispensable ethical category, for there surely must be something, some basic and indisputable morality, consisting of the norms which make possible the mere conservation of life.

The ecology debate, too, leads us to suspect that there must be certain fundamental rules in our relations with creation. It is this fundamentally life-preserving quality of the Decalogue which links it with Natural Law. Dietrich Bonhoeffer, in his *Ethics*, therefore called the decalogue the "Law of Life," for "failure to observe the second table (of the Decalogue) destroys life. The task of protecting life will itself lead to observance of the second table" (i.e., the commandments which rule inter-human relationships) (*Ethics*, E.T. 1955, Fontana 1964, p.341). Goodness or righteousness is what is right and fit for creation; the good is what will correspond to the laws in creation and so will preserve and promote life.

The life-sustaining quality of the Natural Law expressed in the Decalogue brings us full circle, for this is exactly what was said of the Ten Commandments when they were originally revealed: Keep them, so that you may live. The commandments are God's principles for sustaining his creation. With these commandments, God articulates the law of life of his creatures. Because they define what will promote life, the commandments are an extraordinary blessing for every living creature. They lay out, as it were, the space in which human life will blossom. Whatever action is taken beyond these borders will—sooner or later—destroy life.

So the Sabbath commandment, for instance, is a great gift: You may rest on the seventh day. "Remember the Sabbath day, to keep it holy," is at the same time liberation from the burden of the working day, freedom from urge and anxiety. After liberation from the ceaseless toil in Egypt, after the liberation from foreign rule, Israel (and we all) shall not again fall prey to our own or others' wrong and destructive desires and ambitions.

Every other commandment similarly represents liberation from a dangerous and destructive temptation: In each instance I learn that I no longer need to search for the truth and fulfillment of my life. The fullness of life will certainly not be found in theft or with the wife or husband of someone else.

The Ten Commandments, then, are to the field of ethics what an area-code is to telephoning: They spare us the trouble and anguish of experimenting endlessly among the whole "keyboard" of human possibilities, most of which do not promote life and community at all.

Sociologists seem to confirm the "wisdom" (Dt. 4:6) of the pre- or advance-ordering of morality by God. Individuals would be overwhelmed by the effort to decide their actions each time from scratch, from the full range of what is conceivable or physically possible. The field or "area code" defined by the commandments is the place where life will prosper. That is why he who has received the commandments can be so joyful about them (Ps. 119), why he can sing "he maketh me lie down in green pastures" (Ps. 23:2).

What, after all, is the aim of those who declare the Decalogue out of date? Do they wish to give freedom to gossip and theft? Do they expect by this to serve progress and further life? Is adultery ever good? For whom? Also for the deceived party? Of course, those who consider the Decalogue out of date do not wish to promote evil. But where the Decalogue is not, there also the other good things bestowed by God are not. This goes both for creation and for redemption, and is true for all people—not just for

Christians or Jews. This is how Luther is said to have put it: "He who breaks one of the commandments is like a man who bows too far out of a fourth floor window: He'll fall down and surely break his neck, be he Turk, Jew, Gentile or Christian."

For all humankind, then, the commandments are the proper ground where the house must be built and nowhere else. This the Creator has decided. And this lot will prove to be a sound place. There is no morass beneath it which cannot be fathomed, and no shifting sands, only firm ground and solid rock. A house built on these foundations will weather the crises of history. From other foundations one will have to move again and again, for they will not stand firm indefinitely.

God's commandments, then, promote life. This is what Deuteronomy says and experience confirms. However, we must not think of this truth as an impersonal law which functions independently of God. Rather, we should understand that it is the Lord who *makes* you live. You cannot grasp life with your own hands. It is in the hands of the living God. Godless, immanent ethical solutions, however well-intentioned, are always prey to the will of humans which can quickly change from good to bad. Independent of God's commandments, people may—even tomorrow—act and argue quite differently from today.

This means, moreover, that God's commandments must determine what is beneficial. The argument often heard today that we ought to keep the Decalogue not as commandments from God but as rules pertaining to the benefit of man, opens the door to the corruption of ethics. It is God's authority which says "this is good." Human insight in the end will come to the same conclusion but often, before the final result of an action is evident, great damage has been done. Therefore, we must reject the fashionable demand today for an experimental ethics ("inductive approach," as J.A.T. Robinson calls it in *Christian Freedom in a Permissive Society*, 1970, p.31) which claims the right of everyone to discover his own ethics by trial and error. Against this it has to be remembered that often it is the other person who suffers the damage brought about by my deviation from the Decalogue. Consequently, I may learn nothing, unless the other person, the victim of my experiment in ethics, takes revenge. In this way I may come to learn painfully what God's commandments sought to teach me without the rod, namely the contents of the "golden rule": "All things whatsoever you would that men should do to you, do you even so to them" (Mt. 7:12). The Decalogue is nothing other than an exposition of the golden rule. As such, it belongs as much to the town hall as the pulpit.

We have stated before that the Ten Commandments are being surpassed by *Christian* ethics on the road to righteousness. The Ten Commandments are like the guard-rails of a road through a swamp or along a precipice. The rail itself is not the aim of the journey. And no one would wish to approach his destination with steering wheel locked, directed only by the painful scraping of the car along the rail. What you need instead is inside control—a steering wheel. The Ten Commandments are standards, but they are not the aim. They are the framework, but by no means the realization of God's plan in the world.

God's aim and our calling and destiny is the perfection of man according to the image of Christ. The aim is a kingdom of justice in the world where God's will is being done, for the benefit of his Creation. The Decalogue is the framework for the accomplishment of this. But in a given situation, who or what will tell us what is the right thing to do out of a half of dozen good and permitted possibilities? If the Decalogue resembled the area codes what, as it were, decides the individual number? Because the Ten Commandments as *law* only describe the scene of life negatively ("Thou shalt not..."), it still needs to be filled—we must get the particular number elsewhere. Romans 13:10 needs to be understood in this way ("Love is the fulfillment of the law") as does Romans 8:4, which is a fascinating and very comprehensive description of the process of Christian ethics: Christ came "in order that the righteous requirements of the law might be fully met in us who do not live according to our sinful nature but according to the Spirit."

Here we touch on that large chapter of Christian ethics which goes beyond the mere observance of the commandments. Here, too, it is legitimate to demand a *situation ethics*, because the Decalogue will never tell you positively what is to be done in a given situation. Indeed, we may constantly expect—from the Holy Spirit—a Christian "new morality," to use the notorious phrase coined by Joseph Fletcher and Bishop J.A.T. Robinson. However, these authors used the demand for an ethics which is relevant to the situation in order to oust the Decalogue from Christian ethics. That is why Robinson in his *Honest to God* (London: SCM, 1963) argued that nothing was wrong in itself; all depends on the situation; nothing was prescribed except love. The Decalogue was removed from ethics because of its absolute and eternally-valid demands. The so-called "new morality" of the sixties maneuvered itself into an antithesis of law and love which certainly does not represent the spirit and substance or the wording of the New Testament.

The "new morality's" replacing of the stiff commandments with a flexible ethics of the situation is a reaction against much of traditional church morality which reduced the instruction of the living God to the Ten Commandments and perhaps a few ordinances for masters and servants, husband and wives, parents and children. Does God still speak and guide today? "No" seems to be the answer of traditional ethics. Traditional dogmatics rightly rejected a view of God as Deism, which patterned him after a watchmaker who has made a clock and set it in motion, and then has left it to run by itself. But in ethics, these same theologians seem to confess a God who, after having pronounced the commandments, left the scene and is now silent. Hence, there is a certain historic justification for the rebellion of the new morality.

In the New Testament, however, the Ten Commandments are not abolished, they are surpassed, and thus fulfilled. Christians must reject Fletcher's and Robinson's antithesis of law and love, and their consequent dismissal of the law. This is not compatible with Paul's phrase, "love fulfills the law." Instead, they read Paul as if he had said, "love bypasses the law." We must not succumb to a dichotomy of law and love. Christian ethics involves not the alternative of law or freedom, but the synthesis of law and spirit.

The same idea lies behind Luther's much-quoted statement: "A Christian will create new decalogues." Within its original context, it has a meaning completely different from that which is implied by those who use it to argue that Christians are exempt from and beyond the Ten Commandments. The argument in Luther actually runs like this:

> "We will make new decalogues...and these decalogues are clearer than the Decalogue of Moses.... For when the Gentiles in the very rottenness of their nature still could speak of God and were a law to themselves, (Romans 2), how much more can Paul or a perfect Christian full of the Spirit design a decalogue and judge everything in the best way.... However, as for the time being we are unequal in the spirit, and the flesh is hostile to the spirit, it is necessary, also because of the sectarians, to stick to the certain commandments and writings of the apostles so that the Church may not be torn into pieces. For we are not all apostles who by certain providence of God have been sent to us as infallible teachers. Therefore not they, but we may go astray and fall in the faith." (Luther, in the disputation On Faith, Nov. 11, 1535).

The Spirit and Scripture are consonant because both are the Word of the same God. It is in the field defined by the Decalogue —and nowhere else—that God will continue to instruct, prohibit and command. Because the Ten Commandments are the appointed place for the dialogue and communication of God and man, they remain valid for all of us.

I conclude with a quotation from a famous sermon of Martin Luther's on Matthew 22:36-46:

> *"Therefore learn, who can learn, and learn well, so that we may know, first the Ten Commandments, what we owe to God. For if we do not know this, then we know nothing and will not inquire about Christ in the least...The Law...must show me what my loss and disease are, or I will never ask for the physician and his help"* (Sermon on the 18th Sunday after trinity, from his Church Postil).

Law and gospel must go together.

AUTHOR INDEX

Adams, J.	101
Akiba, Rabbi	36
Ambrose	13
Amery, Jan	100
Antiochus	74
Aquinas, Thomas	15, 24, 46, 76-77
Aristotle	37, 38, 46
Augustine	12-13, 97
Bakunin, Michael	90
Bally, Gustav	85
Barnabas, Letter of	11
Barth, Karl	18, 38, 78, 129-130, 131
Baumgartner	80
Bernard of Clairvaux	15
Bonaventura	15
Bonhoeffer, Dietrich	131
Brunner, Emil	19, 38
Buber, Martin	56
Calvin, Jean	17, 20, 22, 24, 26, 29, 54, 56, 57, 64, 66, 76-77, 89, 91, 92, 117
Camus, Albert	78
Childs, Brevard	8
Chrysostom	115
Cicero	13
Clement of Alexandria	12
Edmund of Canterbury	15

Feuerbach, Ludvig	57
Fletcher, Joseph	19, 99, 134
Frankl, Victor	11
Heine, Heinrich	36
Hillel, Rabbi	107
Hitler, Adolf	100
Irenaeus	12
Jeremias, Joachim	40, 84
Jerome	12, 13, 14
Kant, Immanuel	37, 45
Kierkegaard, Soren	19
Lochman, Jan M.	119
Luther, Martin	16-17, 22, 37-38, 64, 76, 89, 91, 92, 93, 115, 119, 122, 127, 130, 135
Marx, Karl	33, 57
Melanchthon	22
Morgenthaler, Dr.	98
Nietzsche, Freidrich	2
Origen	12
Pliny	77
de Quervain, Alfred	128
Reade, Charles	34
Ritschl, Albert	18
Robinson, J.A.T.	19, 133, 134
Schleiermacher, Friedrich	18, 38, 56
Spock, Dr.	85
Stamm, J.J.	93
Unwin, J.E.	104-105
Wollebius, Johannes	20, 24

Scripture Index

Old Testament

Genesis

1:23	96	20:4-6	51	31:14, 15	72
1:27-28	107	20:5	52	31:16	73
2:2-3	70	20:6	43	31:17	70
2:3	70	20:7	59	31:18	7
3:17	71	20:8-11	69	32	33, 52, 54
9:5-6	93	20:9	70	32:26-29	84
14:14-26	113	20:10	70, 72	34:17	51
24	108	20:13	20, 93, 94	34:21	71
27:11	111	20:17	121	34:28	7
29:16-30	104	20:22-24	52	35:2, 3	72
29:20	108	20:23	53	36:38	7
29:23 ff	111	20:24	54		
30:25 ff	111	21-23	8, 23	*Leviticus*	
41:55	83	21:2	24	17-26	51
44	111	21:12-17	8	19	9
44:9	111	21:15	79	19:3	80
		21:15	79	19:7	94
Exodus		21:17	24, 79	19:12	59
4:22	39	22:1, 4, 7	111	19:16	118
3:14	60	22:20	29	19:18	10, 94, 118
14:31	80	22:21	24		
16:19	72	23:11	111	19:30	71
16:28-29	72	23:12	71	19:32	80
19:4	39	23:12-13	8-9	20:9	79
20	8, 29	23:13	29	20:10 ff	103
20:1	7	24:7	29	24:10-16	61
20:2	127	24:10	61	24:16	59
20:3-17	7	24:11	61	25	114
20:3	29	25:21	7	25:14	112

25:43, 53	86	12:5 f	60	*1 Kings*	
26:1	51	14:1	39	8:27	54
26:2	71	14:28	114	8:56	78
27:2-3	80	17:3	30	19:10	31
		19:1-13	93	21	121
Numbers		19:16-21	118	21:19	93
15:32-36	72	20:7	108		
18:21-24	114	21:18-21	79	*2 Kings*	
30:2	66	22:22	103	23:24	53
35:9-34	93	22:23	103		
		23:24	103, 112	*2 Chronicles*	
Deuteronomy		22:25-27	103	5:10	7
1:31	39	23:25	74	6:11	7
3:21	54	24:1	104, 107	23:17	53
4	8	24:5	108	28:2	52
4:1-2	126	24:15	111	33:3	52
4:6	130, 132	26:12	114	34:3-4	53
4:13	7	27:15	52	36:21	70
4:14	8	27:16	79		
4:15-19	52	30:10	32	*Ezra*	
4:23-25	52	31	8	3	87
4:24	30	33:3	39	3:17-21	87
4:25-26	52	33:9	84	7:20	52
4:27	52			22:6	9
4:34	127	*Joshua*		34	87, 88
5	29	4:14	80	36:22 ff	64
5:6-21	7	7:19	65		
5:7	29	7:21	121	*Nehemiah*	
5:8-10	51	22:5	31	10:31	73
5:9b	52	23:7	30	13:15	73
5:11	59	24:23	30		
5:12-15	69, 71			*Job*	
5:18	103	*Judges*		5:21	118
5:20	117	5:31	43	31:1	104, 105
5:21	121	17:4	52	31:7	104
6:4 5	8				
6:5	31, 32, 43	*1 Samuel*		*Psalms*	
6:6-9	8	1:8	108	5:11-12	62
6:13	62, 65, 66	3:10	32	8:3	54
6:20	126	3:13	82	9:2	61, 62
6:21-25	126	5:1-4	36	9:38	61
6:13	32	15:22	30	14:1-3	56, 57
7:25	121			15	10
9:11	7	*2 Samuel*		18:1, 2	44
9:15	7	12:5, 6	112	18:49	62
10:5	7	12:11	104	19	44
11:28	30	16:14	70	20:1b	60
12:5	54	23:15	121	22:22	62

23:2	132	*Isaiah*		2:11	73	
24	10	1:13	73	2:19	104	
24:4	59	5:12	54	2:19-20	40	
26:8	44	10:1-3	112	4:2	9	
33:21	62	11:2	14	4:2-6	112	
40:17	44	40:18-25	52	6:4	43	
46:10	76	42:17	52	6:6	44	
50:15	62	43:4	39	11:1	39	
50:18-20	9	44:6-23	52	13:4	30	
53:2-4	56	44:16-17	33			
63:3	56	49:15	39	*Joel*		
63:11	62, 65	50:1	40	2:32	62	
69:9	31	50:4	47			
70:5	44, 108	58	114	*Amos*		
75:1	60	58:13	72	5:27	52	
76:1	60	58:13ff	73	8:4-6	112	
81:6	71	62:5	40	8:5	73	
85:8a	47	63:9	39			
86:7	56	64:4	45	*Micah*		
96:8	62			7:6	83	
97:7	52	*Jeremiah*				
102:21-22	62	3:1, 2	40	*Habakkuk*		
103:1	62	3:19-20	43	1:16	30	
106:14	121	7:6-9	9			
106:19-21	52	7:9	93	*Malachi*		
106:20	53	7:18	30	1:2	39	
115:1	64	10:3 ff	33	2:15b	104	
115:4-8	33	17:21-23	73	2:16	40	
119	132	17:24 ff	73	3:8	114	
119:2	32	22:13	86	4:2	62	
119:58	32	29:13-14	32	4:4-6	81	
		31:3	39			
Proverbs		31:9	43			
1:8	80	31:20	39			
3:7	80					
6:25	122	*Ezekiel*				
10:3b	113	9:4	7			
11:26	112	20:12	73			
13:4	123	20:13	73			
15:15	80	20:20	73			
19:17	114	22:8	73			
19:26	79					
20:17	112	*Daniel*				
20:20	79	6:10	54			
21:25	123					
23:22	80	*Hosea*				
31:10	108	2:5	43			
		2:7	40			

New Testament

Matthew		19:16-22	14	6:6	77
4:10	32, 66	19:18	128	6:35-38	61
5	14, 37,	19:19	81	7:12-16	81
	106	19:21	12	7:34	41
5-7	9	20:28	88	7:36-50	44
5:17	128	22:34 ff	43	8:3	25
5:18-20	129	22:36-46	135	10:30-37	26
5:20	12, 13, 87	22:37	32	11:5-8	41
5:21	9, 94	22:37-39	32	11:11	82
5:23	95	23:1-4	129	11:25	95
5:27	9	23:9	84	11:42	44
5:27-30	105	23:25	112	12:4	41
5:28	122	24:45	88	12:15	113
5:32	106	25	123	12:48	89
5:33-37	9, 66	25:14-30	114	12:49	124
5:43	96	25:25 ff	114	13:10-17	74
5:45	39	25:31-36	14	13:15	75
6:9-13	63	25:31-46	94	13:15-17	75
6:32	123	25:34-46	25	14:26	84
6:33	123	26:65	61	15	83, 95, 99
7:7	123	26:74	65	15:11-32	40, 82
7:12	11, 21, 23,	27:46	63	15:18-19	48
	25, 133			16:13	31, 106
10:21	83	*Mark*		18:13	47
10:33	63	1:35	47	18:29	84
10:33-34	83	2:23-28	74	19	25
10:37	84	2:27	70	23:34	96
11:12	124	3:1-6	74		
11:20-26	46	3:4	26, 95	*John*	
12:1	75	4:19	34	1:48	57
12:46	83	6:18	89	2:3	83
12:50	84	7:10	81	2:5	83
15:2	128	7:22	113	2:16	77
15:4	81	10:11	106	3:16	42
15:4-6	10	12:28-34	44	4:19-24	69
15:19	10, 11, 23,	14:36	63	4:21-24	55
	106, 112	14:55-50	118	4:24	55
18:15-16	118			5:12	66
18:17	118	*Luke*		5:18	61
18:21, 22	95	1:38	49	5:30	47, 83
19	10, 14, 23,	1:47	49	7:53-8:11	105
	107	2:49	77, 83	8:26	61
19:3	107	2:51	83	8:40	61
19:3	107	3:11	114	8:42	44
19:9	106	4:16	77	9:1	66
19:11	12	6:5	76	9:24	65

10:10	115	*Romans*		7:13-15	107
10:33	61	1:11	114	7:15	107
11:11	41	1:21-23	53	7:19	76
11:36	41	1:25	53	8:1-3	45
12:45	55	1:30	81	8:4	60
13:8-10	76	2	135	8:6	31, 32
13:12-17	88	2:14-15	12, 130,	10:14	31
14:15	31		131	10:24	96
14:21	45	2:18	4	12:2	31
15:9	43	3:1-12	57	13:13	32
15:10	31	3:20	22	16:2	77
15:14	41	5:5	13, 42	16:15	87
17:6	60	5:8	42	16:19	109
17:26	60	8:4	134	16:22	46
19:26-27	84	8:15	45, 63		
		8:28	43, 97	*2 Corinthians*	
Acts		8:29	57	1:23	66
1:1	55	8:35	42	1:24	88
2:1	77	10:10	63	3:17	55
2:21	62	10:13	62	3:18	57
2:37	2	11:11-24	42	4:18	55
4:12	60	11:17	128	5:10	2, 78
4:32-35	114	11:28	40	5:14	42
5:27	91	12:8	114	5:15	32, 48
5:29	84	12:10	96	8-9	114
7:59	96	13	23, 90, 91	8:14	114
8	48	13:1	88	12:14	82
8:37	32	13:4	93		
9	48	13:8-10	11, 23	*Galatians*	
9:14	63	13:9	10, 11	2:20	43, 76
9:15	63	13:10	134	3:13	105
10:19	27	15:2	96	3:14	128
12:12	25, 85	15:17	96	3:26	42
15:20	106	16:2-14	109	3:27	86
16:6-10	23			4:6	45, 63
16:34	85	*1 Corinthians*		4:8	31
17:2	77	1:2	63	5:20	31, 94
17:16	31	2:9	45	6:15	76
17:24-29	53	2:17	88		
18:2	109	4:15	84	*Ephesians*	
18:26	109	5:7	24	2:4	42
19:17	62	6	26	2:11-13	42
19:35	53	6:9	31, 112	3:14-15	41
20	87	6:9-11	107	4-6	25
20:33-34	123	6:10	113	4:9	78
20:35	115, 123	6:11b	63	4:25	118
22:16b	63	7	14	4:26	95

4:28	112, 114	*1 Timothy*		4:4	46
4:32	108	1:5	11, 85	4:17	76
5	40	1:8-10	11, 23	5:1-6	113
5:5	31, 113	1:9	11, 81	5:12	67
5:20	62	5:4	81, 82		
5:21-33	108	5:8	81, 82	*1 Peter*	
6	82	5:17	87	1:8	45, 55
6:1-4	81	6:1	64	1:13	32
6:2	81	6:6-10	123	1:17	63
6:4	82	6:9	88	1:23	41
6:5-8	86	6:10	113	2:23 ff	86
6:9	86	6:13	66	4:11	62
6:24	46			4:15	112
		2 Timothy		5:1-4	88
Philippians		2:19b	64	5:7	35
2	96	2:22	63		
2:3	115	3:2	81	*2 Peter*	
2:4	96, 115	4:10	46	2:14	106
2:5-11	96	4:18	45		
2:6	115	4:19	109	*1 John*	
2:9	60			2:5	46
4:6	35	*Titus*		3:1	42
		2:7	87	3:11-24	42
Colossians		2:14	2	3:13	94
1:15	55			4:11	42
3	82	*Philemon*		4:16b	43
3:1-2	124	1:16	86	4:19	43
3:5	113			4:20	95
3:9-10	118	*Hebrews*		5:2	45
3:10	57	4:14	24	5:21	31
3:12	42	6	114		
3:17	64	6:16	65	*Revelation*	
3:20	82	9:27	89	13:14 ff	53
3:22-25	86	10:1-14	24		
4:1	86	11:1	55		
		12:7	82		
1 Thessalonians		12:29	30		
1:4	42	13:5	123		
2:8	114	13:17	87		
2:11	82				
4:6	112	*James*			
5:12	87	2:14-17	114		
		3:1	87		
2 Thessalonians		3:1-11	117		
1:12	62	4:1-2	122		
3:5	46	4:2	122		
3:11-12	114	4:3	123		

Apocrypha

Wisdom of Solomon		*Ecclesiasticus*		*Tobit*	
8:7	13	3	80	2:9	14
13:10-19	52	23:9	65		
				Judith	
				8:6	72

Subject Index

Abortion	96 ff
Adiaphora	4
Adultery	36, 103 ff
Anarchism	90 f
Antichrist	53
Authority,	
business	86
church	87 f
parents	85 f
state	88 ff
Ceremonial law	24
Civil law	24, 26
Commandment of Love	10, 12 f, 19, 23, 25
Confessional Mirror	15, 16
Conversion	26
Counsels of Perfection	12 f, 14, 15
Covenant, the Book of the	29
Coveting	112 f, 121 f
Creation ethics	25 f, 27
Diaphora	4
Divorce	104, 106 f
Duty	13

Ethic of avoidance	75 f
Ethics of salvation	26 f
Euthanasia	100
Family	81 ff
Fetish	50
Forgivness	95 f
Friendship	41 ff
Golden Rule, the	11, 21, 25, 26
Government, resistance of	91 f
Holiness	2
Homosexuality	35, 103, 107
Humanity, true	45
Idolatry	33 f, 51 ff
Image	55 ff
Individuality	3
Intolerant, God as	36
Kingdom of God	123 f
Law, the three-fold use of	9, 22
Lawlessness	27
Love for God	37 ff, 43 ff
Marriage	107 f
Mercy, Works of	14, 26, 94, 114
Missions	3, 27
Monolatry	30
Natural Law	4, 12, 13, 18, 23, 25 f, 89
Oath	65 ff
Obedience	47 ff
Prayer	46 f
Perfection	13
Relativism	4 f, 70
Sanctify	47 ff
Secularism	3, 101
Sermon on the Mount	12, 16, 23, 94, 128
Situational ethics	19
Suicide	100 f

Sunday	77 f
Synecdoche	21
Talion formula	94
Theft	111 ff
Virtue	13 ff, 21
Wealth	113

Printed in the United States
19178LVS00003B/7-15